Undefeated

The Extraordinary Life and Death of
Lt. Col. Jack Sherwood Kelly
VC, CMG, DSO

by
Philip Bujak

Ed. J.C. & S.C. Gough

By The Same Author:

Norfolk and Suffolk in The Great War (Cont.) (1988)

Attleborough - The Evolution of a Town (1990)

Montessori Around The World in 100 years (2007)

Printed in England by Abbey Printers (Devon) Ltd.
Newton Abbot, TQ12 2DF.   Tel: 44 (0)1626 201212.

First published in Great Britain in 2008 by Forster Consulting.

ISBN: 0-9551902-2-3   978-0-9551902-2-3

About The Author

Philip was born in February 1960. His mother comes from a long established rural Norfolk family providing for the cider making industry with four great uncles who served in The Norfolk Regiment during The Great War - his namesake was the first British soldier to die of his wounds in this country having been wounded at Mons in August 1914. His father was born in Wejherowo, Poland in 1919 and was a regular soldier serving in the Polish Army as a signals officer and was wounded at Monte Cassino with the 3rd Carpathian Division, 2nd Polish Corps. He was decorated with The Cross of Valour in 1945. Philip's brother Edward is Associate Professor of English History at Harlaxton College in Lincolnshire.

Philip was educated at both state and independent schools and, after a period in The Junior Leaders Regiment, chose to read English and European Political History at The University of East Anglia between 1979 and 1982 going on to pursue a highly successful career in teaching. Having taught History at Wymondham College, Philip moved to Langley School in Norfolk (450 pupils Co-Ed) as Head of History and between 1985 and 1994 was a boarding boys Housemaster of Beauchamp House. In 1994 Philip was appointed Headmaster of Stover School for Girls (540 pupils 3-18) where he had a significant impact on enlarging the school and placing it at the forefront of schools in Devon. In 2004 Philip was appointed Chief Executive of The Montessori St Nicholas Charity and now leads the Montessori movement across the United Kingdom having created the Montessori Schools Association which now numbers 547 schools in membership and represents over 30,000 children.

In his youth Philip represented Norfolk and Eastern Counties at soccer and Athletics, was a junior apprentice footballer with Norwich City, represented University at both badminton and rugby and played Hockey for The Territorial Army. Philip was commissioned into 6th (V) Battalion The Royal Anglian Regiment in 1983. In the late 1980's and early 1990's Philip wrote a series of articles on Norfolk local history and published his first book. He is a keen observer of the human condition, an active supporter of charitable causes and counts friendship as one of his greatest joys along with his two children Alexander and Eleanor.

Dedication

To Alex and Eleanor and all my friends.

Acknowledgements

The collecting of information and development of my understanding of Jack in order to write this book has crossed two decades. Along the way I have been supported and helped by so many individuals that time and again my faith in the intrinsic goodness of people, what some would call Christian Spirit, has been rebuilt when in so many other ways it has been let down. In paying tribute to some of the builders here I recognise that many have since passed away.

To my long suffering immediate family Anne, Alex and my typist Eleanor who have heard the name Jack Kelly so often he must seem like a long lost relation. To HCDK who gave me the final push to finish what had become a companion rather than a book and to my mother Phyliss whose idea it was to record Jack's life in the first place.

Without the help of John Kelly of Walmer South Africa, whom I had the pleasure to once meet, I would not have had access to many of the sources that have been used to place Jack in the timetable of his life and thank you to Julia and Peter Walsh of New South Wales who, in a chance meeting, provided much of the information on Nellie and Mount Oriel; Burgess Winter whose sense of the Irish temperament provided a much needed empathy with the inherent dangers of Irish passion; Mr Peter Long of Farnham who researched the wedding of Nellie's younger sister and the late Mr. W.M. Morris who, having seen an article in the Eastern Daily Press, called me to come and see him and sat in his chair telling me what he had seen of Jack as a young solicitor's clerk, provided me with a ray of insight into the voice and character of the man himself.

The following public bodies were immensely helpful in providing source material and photographs on which to build a chronology of events: The South African National Museum of Military History, The British Library, The Victoria Cross and George Cross Association, The Eastern Daily Press, The Daily Express, The National Army Museum, The National Archives in Kew, The Imperial War Museum and The National Newspaper Library. Without the help of the various regimental museums and records I would not have been able to chart Jack's journey through the British Army most notably The Royal Norfolk Regiment who came up trumps; The Royal Hampshire Regiment, especially Lt. Col. C.D. Darroch DL who provided valuable photographs of Jack and members of the 2nd Battalion in North Russia; The Suffolk and Norfolk Yeomanry Trust and especially Lt. Col. J.H. Boag OBE, MC, TD, DL and the Regimental Records of The Kings Own Scottish Borderers.

A huge thank you to Andy and Julie Penny of Abbey Printers in Newton Abbot for their support in the design and printing of this book. Finally to three people who I am proud to call friends who encouraged me to publish this book. Mr Tim Key of Devon who once was rash enough to say that I could write and to Sue and John Gough of Shropshire who offered to proof read the text and offered their own personal and very relevant insights into life and the man.

Contents

CHAPTER 1

'A man of character in peace is a man of courage in war'.
- General Sir James Glover

THE IMPERIAL ADVENTURE - PART ONE: FINDING THE MAN, 1830-1902

A tombstone in a quiet Surrey cemetery, neglected for many years and unvisited for even more, with an inscription all but obscured by decay, lichen and dirt is the only memorial to a man whose extraordinary life touched that of one of the 20th century's most iconic figures and could, perhaps should, have brought about his ruin.

Closer examination of the inscription reveals the name John Sherwood Kelly and the evocative letters 'V.C.' and the account of his relatively short life takes one in a headlong dash from the South African veldt to the deserts of Somalia, from the beaches of Gallipoli to the killing fields of Northern France and from the frozen wastes of Northern Russia to the steaming jungles of Bolivia. To the historian this itinerary provides the clue to Jack Kelly's series of interactions with the developing political career of Winston Spencer Churchill. To the psychologist the story of Jack's early years may well contain the clues to a man of volcanic energies but equally powerful emotions and contradictions.

Jack's grandfather James Kelly was a native of Newbridge in County Kildare, Ireland. A regular soldier, James Kelly had served in the British Army throughout the 1840's and at the time of the birth of his son John James Kelly on 4th June 1850, he was serving in The Crimea - taking part and surviving The Charge of the Light Brigade at Balaclava in October 1854. As a young man John Kelly subsequently saw a better future for his family overseas staking a claim in one of the many colonies rather than returning to England or an impoverished and starving Ireland and to start his civilian life. How South Africa became the focus of his attention we do not know, but during the 1860's the family emigrated from Ireland and established itself in The Cape region of South Africa where John James Kelly settled his family in Queenstown, Cape Colony, at some point in the early 1870s. On the 30th July 1877 he married Emily Jane Didcott who had been born in Winchester in June 1858. This young couple aged twenty-seven and nineteen years old respectively, very quickly began what was to become a family of ten children with Emily Nuovo Abele Kelly being born on 18th May 1878 in Queenstown. Two years later Emily gave birth to twin boys - John Sherwood Kelly and Hurbert Henry Kelly. The family then moved to Buffle Doorns where another brother and sister were added between 1880 and 1882. We will never know why John and Emily then decided to move north east into the far more rugged yet beautiful interior of the Transkai where they would live for the rest of their lives in the shadow of Mount Frere - and here a further five children were added to the family.

For John James Kelly this unforgiving landscape would be where he was to spend the rest of his life through to his death August 18th, 1926. The interior of South Africa was populated by numerous tribes, many of them Zulu, which meant it was essential to try to assimilate and work with people who for the most part did not reject the new technology and progress that the colonists brought with them. There were many exceptions of course but it was down largely to people such as John James Kelly who, after his father's death, became the local Law Agent. This was a vital role as he acted as arbiter, enforcer and representative of British law and at times British policy. Clearly such men could have achieved only a fraction of what they actually did had they not discovered some exceptional women to depend on to run and build their families.

John James Kelly was a short, strong and determined man. His Irish temperament served him well at times and not so well at others and undoubtedly he had to give a high regard to the views of his wife. It is however so important that we understand his character as it is in his undoubted influences over his children that we will learn so much more about the experiences, values and emotions that drove one of his sons - Jack Kelly. Again in this way, we can ourselves stand a better chance of standing back dispassionately and evaluating Jack as an individual and the choices that he made in later life.

In a small and undated work entitled 'The Life and People of Lady Frere' we gain a valuable insight into the life of this small colonial community and the role played in it by Jack's father John James for example:

"His (John James Kelly) true Irish temperament revealed itself in his courage at all times, whether it be courage to speak up in the defence of his fellow man or courage to save the lives of those in distress. He also had the courage to go against those whom he thought had stepped out of line and then his attack was relentless even though they were his friends."

If there is one part of this entire book that needs remembering in regards to the life and actions of Jack Kelly then this is it. It could have been written about him and especially that concerned with the "relentless" pursuit of what he perceived to be those who were perverting justice - even to the point of his own self destruction. In this respect more than any other we immediately have a strong lead into the character that shaped Jack Kelly's perceptions of life, values and actions - his father.

'The Life and People of Lady Frere' goes on to elaborate numerous instances surrounding the life of the township and its inhabitants and the role John James Kelly played in it. For example we read that the local community church was used by a different religious denomination each Sunday for their own form of worship - those who were simply 'Christian' did of course attend every week. Once a month the wagons and carts would bring in from all over the area the Boer families of The Dutch Reformed Church who would arrive for their 'Nagmaal' bringing their own pots, kettles and foods to cook their communal lunch in a room they had booked at the back of the Lady Frere Hotel - "Fathers, mothers, grannies, grandfathers, aunts, uncles and children spilled out of black buggies and trooped in orderly fashion." (1)

The whole area was of course also a boiling pot of potential hazards and tribal friction which it was often the lot of John James Kelly to untangle and defuse. He was regularly critical of the local Xhosa tribes people who could not be relied upon to observe the necessary self restraint needed for groups of people from different cultures to live together but in some respects this was understandable - it was their land. Aggression and even localised rebellion were always simmering beneath the surface. However, John James Kelly built a reputation amongst all groups for being a firm but very fair judge of circumstance and as we already know he was not afraid to speak up for the most influential white man or the most humble native of the area - "he never deviated from giving each and every individual his services and a fair hearing." Blending the local tribal laws and customs which had sufficed for centuries with the new 'white man's' laws must have been a tremendously difficult task if one wanted to achieve the desired result not through force of arms but through consensus.

A good example comes with the passing of the Glen Gray Act when Kelly even challenged Cecil Rhodes in parliament over what he saw as the unfair implementation of this law. He reminded the government that their high handedness was undermining the efforts of all those in the rural areas trying to work with the local people and that the Act needed to consider tribal laws and customs and not just impose central government's views on the people. Kelly here was representing the Xhosa people who were affected by this new legislation and he went on to openly criticise Rhodes for misrepresenting the facts about events in the Glen Gray District. Interestingly, John Kelly made this open attack by writing to 'The Cape Argus' which published his letters across South Africa. Such an open and courageous style was both admirable but also dangerous but again it is something that no doubt had an impact on his son Jack who saw what bravery his father was able to show in the face of considerable odds in the pursuit of justice.

"Here was truly a lone voice in the wilderness, but a man who honestly displayed courage and tenacity unequalled and he did this for the cause of seeing justice and fair play done in all walks of life in the small town of Lady Frere, a mere speck on the map." (2)

Whatever the relationship between John James and his son Jack, we know from this epitaph that both men held justice above all things as sacred - even to the point of their own self destruction.

In the interest of balance our anonymous writer also tells of the impact of the influenza epidemic that affected much of the world in the wake of the First World War. The 'flu took its toll on the region and Lady Frere too was badly affected with over ninety people at one time disabled and dying. A public meeting was held outside the town hall where the Mayor tried to co-ordinate some sort of plan. Only the store remained open and it was here that Kelly heard of the rumour circulating in the district that the white population of Lady Frere were in fact only interested in looking after their own and nothing was being done for the black community. Kelly was incensed and again wrote a long and direct letter to 'The Daily Representative and Free Press' in which he wrote about a group of five ladies - "God Bless them" - who volunteered to make soup in spite of being ill themselves in their own homes with no help and stood from dawn to dusk making 12-15 gallons of soup for daily distribution around the community and surrounding Xhosa villages. Many natives would have surely died but for the delivery of this nourishment by the Native Law Agent who carried the soup in his wagon.

John James Kelly had already also served in the local militia - The Frontier Armed and Mounted Police, which he had joined in 1868. If further evidence of the personal courage of John James Kelly were needed we can look to 6th December 1874 when a strong gale hit the south eastern Cape area on the Transkei coastline. It is not known how Sergeant John Kelly happened to be in this area but perhaps word reached his local Police garrison Headquarters that a ship was aground. An Italian wooden barque of six hundred and ninety tons, the *Nuovo Abele* commanded by Captain Cuneo Francisco, had come to grief and was breaking up off shore having hit some rocks. (3)

The *Nuovo Abele* was on a trip from Batavia to London with a cargo of sugar and a crew of ten. Arriving at the scene and in the midst of the storm it was clear that the ship was going to be smashed and the crew lost unless some way of linking them with the shore could be found. Step forward John Kelly who decided to tie a rope to his waist and swim out to the ship clambering over the rocks and taking the men off one at a time by rope. This was achieved and ten crew members including the Captain were saved. For this heroic rescue John James Kelly was awarded The Royal Society's Bronze Medal for Gallantry for this heroic exploit and, as we have seen, recorded the event personally in the naming of his first born child. The development of policing throughout the colonies and areas of South Africa was a long and by no means comprehensive process but The Cape Mounted Police had replaced the Frontier Police in 1878 and Sergeant John Kelly had remained a member. There were nine Mounted Police Garrisons throughout the Cape with a further three in The Transkai. (4) These units doubled as mounted local police forces composed of volunteers and a mounted militia and their members were expected to support the enforcement of British policy at all times and to join the regular units when and if the time arose.

It was therefore into this life of working with the native populations, heat and hard work and high moral expectations and discipline that Jack Kelly was born on 13th January 1880 in Queenstown, Cape Colony. His twin brother Hurbert Henry was born a few minutes later. It is not known how or when the nickname 'Sherwood' arrived as an established part of Jack's name but he certainly was not christened Sherwood - nor did he ever serve with the Sherwood Foresters as has often been stated. It does however help a biography where so many men and women shared similar family names to have a Sherwood to delineate between the members of the family and so for the purposes of our continuing story we refer to our subject as Jack Sherwood Kelly.

Jack's mother was Emily Jane Didcott who had been born in Winchester on 1st June 1858 and alongside Jack came a number of brothers and sisters - Olive, Edward, Percy, Gertrude, Oswald, Clifford and Ethel to make nine in all. (5)

What we know of Jack as a young boy can be pieced together from a variety of sources. His father was a strong if not overbearing influence. He was a busy man with a large family and many commitments. It is very likely that Jack was a needy child whose emotional needs were provided for by his gentle mother. We already know that his father was a strong and guiding influence with a strong sense of justice, obvious and sometimes outspoken moral and physical courage and considerable qualities of leadership. It is fair to say that Jack inherited all of these characteristics in good measure. Indeed one could extend this by saying that Jack was the product and epitome of his age. At a time where strength of character and vision were vital to exploiting the opportunities available, so were principles of fair play and just as important strength of conviction to see things through to a conclusion. Neither Jack nor his father were interested in playing at politics where economies with the truth and manipulation of circumstance for personal gain were by-words for a successful career. What we lack in our later assessment of Jack's life is any sense of personal emotion. What developed was an heroic figure achieving great deeds, leading a full life but to be cut down and ruined in standing up for justice. But we are not going to see much underneath - the emotional man. For that we have to dwell here in his youth for a moment and look at his relationship with his mother.

As Jack grew up around Lady Frere it is safe to say that he saw more of his mother than his father - not uncommon then and even more common today. His mother therefore was also a key influence on Jack and not just a guiding one but also a protecting and understanding one. Also inherited from his father was a short and hot temper and the frustrations of youth ran deep with Jack Sherwood Kelly as they did for many young men of all ages and times. It is likely that Jack fell foul of his father on many occasions perhaps tempered by his younger brother Edward but equally and more likely by his mother.

However, tragedy struck when Jack was only 12 years of age. The date was August 8th 1892. On that day Emily was driving a horse and cary when the horse bolted. Unable to control it she struggled with the reins in vain until the whole cart was overturned and landed on top of her body killing her outright.

There is no age that can withstand well such a tragic event but there are ages that make an individual stronger than others. At 12 and with a strong and mercurial temper Jack was probably emotionally defenceless. Nothing worse could have happened to this young man and within hours on a single day his entire world was shattered and no-where was there anything to protect him. For a young man for whom justice was one of his watchwords in life, then where was the justice in this? Some measure of his grief can be gleaned from a small plaque in the church in which Emily Jane was buried. It is not from the family of ten or indeed from her husband but from Jack alone and reads:

"She was a true Christian woman, noble, fond, loving affectionate mother and a staunch friend.

Jack, 8th August, 1892."

To the professional eye such words would no doubt indicate a great deal but it is simplicity itself to see that Jack lived in a boyhood world where he needed a friend. How many twelve year old people have we ever met who could call their mothers friends? One is left to wonder on how many occasions Emily mothered Jack as a staunch friend? And why 'staunch?' Was he constantly at odds with his brothers and father - possibly? This made his mother the only person who understood him, what drove him and what made him angry. To lose forever the one person who knew him, was tolerant of his failings when he had so many emotional frailties, would have been completely devastating for Jack. It is to this event every bit as much as the influences of his father that we must attribute much of what happened later and how Jack developed as a person.

But this was not the end. For young men in the interior of South Africa, learning to ride, and ride well despite the size and shape of the horse, was as important as learning to walk. Jack was an especially gifted horseman but then too no doubt were his brothers and sisters. Hardly a year had passed before another tragedy struck the Kelly family. Jack as we have seen was a twin. His brother Hurbert would have grown up every step of the way with Jack and, as is usual with twins, would himself have been closer to Jack than most. On 21st July 1893, a normal, very hot summer's day in Lady Frere, Hurbert was killed after falling from his horse.

How would any of us come to terms with such events? How then a thirteen year-old boy who had in one year lost both his mother and twin brother? How then a boy who already found his relations with people liable to lead to confrontation and who now became a young man with tremendous anger and resentment at the injustice heaped upon him? Maybe he was destined to be alone, fighting his way through life and what did he have to lose if things did not go well? How would or could he show his grief?

According to family recollections it was from this time onwards that Jack 'became unhinged during his teens." His first school was at Grahamstown on the south eastern coast. Of course Jack had to go to school. Victorian public schools were not renowned for their ability to understand emotional problems or even young men. In 1895 and at the age of fifteen Jack was expelled for his uncontrolled anger and behaviour. It would have been a certainty that, whilst being aware of the tragedies that had befallen him, the school would have expected Jack to get on with his lot in life and conform. Although he enjoyed and excelled at the sports offered in school and especially opportunities to ride, he found himself at odds with the often rigid discipline required. Sent home to discuss matters with his father did not help. Indeed it made things worse, for his father, with nine children to bring up, had employed the services of a Miss Selina Collins as governess cum housekeeper to the children and soon after announced that he intended to re-marry, which he did to Miss Collins on 11th April 1894. We will never know the contents of those conversations as neither Jack nor his father left any records and Jack was never to be much of a letter writer. The end result was that although Jack had finished with school his father had not and Jack was enrolled as a boarding pupil at St. Andrew's College. In the meantime his father and step mother provided Jack with three step siblings - Dorothy, Henry and Patrick. (6).

By the age of fourteen therefore Jack had lost his mother whose love knew no boundaries and who was for Jack, one suspects, the only person who understood him by followed by his twin brother the following year. The experience of then seeing his father's remarriage a year after that created such a rollercoaster of emotions in the space of four years that significantly affected the emotional temperament of an insecure and volatile young man. His depths of despair and emotion knew no bounds at the very time that he was sent away to school.

St. Andrew's College had been founded in 1855 and was, in the words of one 'Old Andrean', "a typical Victorian public school, populated by the rough, tough sons of Eastern Cape farmers and equally wealthy sons of Johannesburg businessmen." At the end of 1896 Jack joined the school and it was not to be a complete waste of time. Yet again Jack excelled at sports, as his father had done before him, most notably boxing and riding. There was, one suspects, more to suit Jack's talents and enthusiasm than he had expected, there was also a Cadet Force which in 1890 numbered one hundred and twenty six cadets. With their field grey uniforms and black piping and with officers drawn from the master's common room, this was an attractive diversion from academic studies for Jack. Most schools could boast such units and they further embodied the notion of self defence in a land where native insurrection was as likely as foreign invasion. With relations with the nearby Boer states always strained it is no surprise that a Captain Cherry, when inspecting the unit in 1880, commented "Volunteer forces form a very important part of the colonial army now that we are to expect little aid from Imperial troops in future disturbances."

Unfortunately Jack's career at St. Andrew's was also cut short by expulsion from the college. According to Jean Coulter writing in 1989 "he was not amenable to discipline." (8) At this point we should dwell on another 'troubled youth' who found school not to his liking and preferred the open field to the classroom - one Winston

Spencer Churchill. As has been observed, the lives of these two young men were to become intertwined and it is important to note that they were of a similar disposition if not background. Churchill longed to indulge in activities outside the classroom as opposed to those which 'seemed of the slightest use or interest'. (9)

The year 1896 thus saw Jack Kelly leave school with no qualifications save that of experiencing the style of Victorian discipline that framed the perceptions of generations of British officers, the vast majority of whom would have experienced and, unlike Jack, survived such environments with a regard for discipline unlike any other army.

Avoiding a return home, Jack volunteered for the defence forces being raised to deal with the Matabeleland Rebellion that broke out on the borders of the Transkei in 1896. Inflamed by a local oracle, Matabele warriors set out to raid and murder local white settlers. This was Jack's first taste of real action. We have no details on his involvement save that he was there and no doubt preferred action and riding to school and was awarded The British South Africa Medal (Matabeleland) which was to be the first of his many medal decorations and bars.

Again rather than return home to more friction and strife, Jack decided to follow his fathers lead and enlisted in The Cape Mounted Police. This was a crucial time to make such a decision. Soon after the Matabeleland Rebellion was put down relations were deteriorating fast between Britain and the Boers. The Imperial ambitions of Cecil Rhodes and Sir Alfred Milner were well known and hardly disguised while the increasingly hostile resistance of the Boers led by Transvaal President Paul Kruger made a clash inevitable. The abortive Jameson Raid of 1896 had indeed been a signal flare that conflict was imminent.

Between 1896 and 1899 Jack, as a member of the CMP, filled his time with patrols, arrests and travelling the region on horseback. Later one of his first major roles was to escort Alfred Milner when he visited the Transkei in early 1899. In an article found in an obscure journal called The Nongqai dated February 1918, there is also a reference to Jack being a "rough rider" for the Cape Mounted Police. Although we have no evidence to substantiate this, it would come as no surprise. Rough riders were used to transmit letters and orders into areas with no communications at all and where danger was ever present. Described as "a man of exceptional nerve" such a job would have suited the outstanding horseman that he was and given Jack a lone but exciting role. (10)

Unfortunately a career in the Cape Mounted Police was not to be and, as if to keep up his record of dismissals, Jack was ordered out of the CMP in February 1899. This must have exasperated his father and although we do not know what caused it, it was almost certainly another rebellion against authority. Between 25th February and 17th March his father is known to have written a series of letters trying to find him employment either back in the CMP or with the Native Department. Admitting to Jack's 'nasty temper' and his 'insubordination' but also emphasising his many good points, John James used whatever contacts he could and in July 1899, at the age of nineteen, Jack joined the Native Department in The Cape. Given that the Boer War broke out in September, not even Jack had time to be dismissed before the Cape was thrown into turmoil.

The background to the outbreak of The Boer War was simple enough. President Kruger of The Transvaal wanted to extend his borders but was continually frustrated by the British and most notably Cecil Rhodes. Rhodes had arrived in South Africa in 1870 aged only seventeen and went to Natal for a health cure for Tuberculosis. He became involved in diamond mining and by 1881 he had secured control of virtually all the important diamond mines in and around Kimberly for his company - the DeBeers Corporation, and had become extremely rich. Setting out on a political path, Rhodes became Prime Minister of Cape Colony in 1890. Amongst his many grand designs was linking the Cape with Cairo in Egypt but Transvaal stood in the way. The discovery of gold in the Transvaal in 1886 hugely complicated an already tense situation. If Rhodes was to have his way then the Transvaal would have to become part of the British Empire.

By 1894 it had seemed to Rhodes that the Transvaal was becoming richer than the Cape. It was also becoming less dependent on the Cape as the Boers were able to export and import increasing amounts of goods along their own new railway to secure their complete independence. Kruger was strongly supported by Germany - the Kaiser himself involved in an arms race and imperial struggle with Britain during the 1890's - who was sending him arms and military advisors. The trigger for a sharp deterioration in relations was Kruger's attack on the 'uitlanders' or outsiders. There were tens of thousands of workers mining gold in the Transvaal - many of them British and Kruger was concerned that they would soon outnumber the Boers themselves. Kruger therefore introduced a two tier system where all uitlanders were denied political rights and were taxed more heavily than Boers. Rhodes seized this opportunity to 'protect' British citizens and the British military / political machine engaged itself in overthrowing Kruger.

Unfortunately for Rhodes he made a serious error by plotting with a friend, one Dr. Leander Starr Jameson, to lead a raid into the Transvaal via nearby Bechuanaland which was set to coincide with a rising of uitlanders in Jonahhnesburg. The raid took place in December 1895 but was a complete failure. The British Colonial Secretary, Joseph Chamberlain, disowned all knowledge of the raid and Rhodes was forced to resign. Subsequent research most notably by Elizabeth Longford, suggests that Chamberlain in fact knew all about the raid. This event saw the end of Rhodes' career but the galvanising of the two Boer states into harmony - Transvaal and Orange Free State both now receiving aid from Germany and Kruger even receiving an open telegram from the Kaiser congratulating him on the crushing of the Jameson Raid. For a short while the British abandoned their designs on the Transvaal but the appointment of Sir Alfred Milner as High Commissioner for South Africa was to change all that. In 1898 the uitlanders were 'encouraged' to write to Queen Victoria protesting at their treatment by the Boers. A conference was arranged at Bloemfontain in Orange Free State in June 1899. The belligerent Kruger was in fact prepared to make concessions but these were stretched by Milner into an impossible situation and the conference broke up with no agreement. Milner was not the right man for this job if genuine reconciliation was what was wanted. He was himself an ardent imperialist, impatient and every bit as obstinate as Kruger himself.

Kruger could see what was coming and suggested independent arbitration but also the withdrawal of British troops not just from the borders with the Transvaal but also the Cape. Kruger complained of provocative troop movements on the border and when his ultimatum had failed the Boers had to make a choice - one so often made in history - to await events or take the initiative away from a much stronger enemy by making the first move. This they did and Transvaal and Orange Free State Boers immediately attacked Natal and The Cape. Kruger had played into Milner's hands and as British Prime Minister Lord Salisbury put it long after, *"liberated us from the necessity of explaining to the people of England why we are at war."*

British regiments had been arriving in The Cape for many months as part of a build up of military strength prior to action against the Boers but the British were very badly prepared with only fourteen thousand regular troops in South Africa in July 1899. By October forty-seven thousand troops would arrive under the command of General Redvers Buller but this would be too late to stop the Boers seizing the initiative and throwing sieges around Ladysmith and Mafeking and taking Kimberley altogether.

In Lady Frere, as in hundreds of similar communities, local levies and militias were raised and led by either serving or past serving members of the military. In Lady Frere it was John James Kelly that took on this role building up and leading 'The Lady Frere Company' of the Glen Gray Forces. This rag tag but well intentioned group was formed primarily for the defence of their own area from the Boers. Records pay testimony to his efforts to impose some minimal discipline on his unit with great difficulty - his main task being to issue Defaulter Sheets to nearly every man for breaches of discipline.

Meanwhile the real war had begun and an increasingly vicious war it was going to be and one in which the British army was to lose not only significant numbers of men to disease but also to the new tactics of mounted guerrilla warfare to which they were unaccustomed. It was not unreasonably assumed at the outset of hostilities, that the

British professional soldier would be more than a match for the irregular Boer farmers. But serious defeats at Magersfontein, Stormburg and Colenso were humiliating and the army reserve was called up as it suddenly now seemed that what was going to be a quick victory could end up as humiliating defeat.

The inability of the British troops to pin down rapidly and erase their enemy was soon exposed and it was clear that a new wing of the Army was needed - that of the long range mounted soldier. The majority of the forty-eight thousand or so Boer troops were mounted enabling them to mount lightning attacks and then disappear. They knew the land while the British did not. Lord Roberts was ordered to South Africa as Commander in Chief with the later to be ruthless Kitchener as his Chief of Staff. (11) Between them the tactics changed and became far harder and requests went out throughout the Empire for experienced horsemen to join this imperial struggle. Volunteers began arriving from Canada and Australia while the Cape Mounted Police also provided two thousand men. Altogether twenty-eight thousand men were home grown from the Cape with colourful names such as Montmorency's Scouts, The Transkei Mounted Rifles and The Pioneer Railway Corps. (12) However it was the home grown Imperial Light Horse that stole the show, Churchill's admiration and the headlines and it was to this unit that Jack Kelly volunteered and enlisted having spent barely two months with the Native Department.

Men of the Imperial Light Horse took part in most of the famous and infamous events of the Boer War. In his role as War Correspondent for *The Morning Post* the young Winston Churchill, built up a great admiration for the men of the Light Horse - serving with them in his capacity on a number of occasions and describing them as "the bravest men I have ever seen." (13) Whether Churchill actually met Jack Kelly is a fascinating question and we must assume that he did not but they had already led parallel lives in a number of respects. Both rebelled against school and preferred the outdoor life and adventure, both were strong and stubborn personalities and both were impetuous. Later, although they did not know it in 1899, they were to clash head on in a national scandal that ended Kelly's career but also threatened to bring Churchill down and thus could have changed history dramatically.

The Imperial Light Horse Regiment was formed in September 1899 with the approval of Queen Victoria and was co-ordinated by Col. Aubrey Wools-Sampson, Sir Percy Fitzpatrick and Major Walter "Karri" Davies - all local colonial figures with strong British pedigrees. A call went out for volunteers to join this new regiment and five thousand men put themselves forward with only an elite 440 being selected - Jack Kelly being one. Following the regular troops around in their engagements was dangerous in itself but Churchill also had ample opportunity to watch and work with the men of The Imperial Light Horse. The Light Horse were fast, lightly equipped, well led and brave - this was their kind of warfare and they were a good match for the Boers on most fronts across the huge areas upon which the wars were fought. Two Victoria Crosses were awarded for actions at Elandsgate in October 1899 and over the next two years, Jack Kelly was everywhere he could be as a member of the ILH. We know that at a young age Jack had made a pact with himself that if he ever got the chance he would risk all he had to also win the Victoria Cross - which indeed he was destined to do in 1917. (14) In uniform, armed and able to lead from the front, he realised that here was a vocation in which he could finally and at last express himself. His medals began to accumulate and his first decorations read in order: 'Orange Free State', 'Transvaal', 'Rhodesia' and 'Relief of Mafeking'.

Many miles of hard living and fighting would have gone into this collection of honours and we must remember that we are talking of a young man still only nineteen years old. The war was hard and saw many atrocities to soldiers and civilians alike. The life of the mounted soldier was harsh with endless nights out in the field, torrents of rain, shortage of food, loss of horses, fever, bogs, insects and of course deadly bullets from the Boer sharpshooters. Something of the nature of the fighting can be sensed from these excerpts from the recently unearthed diary of Private Horace Bell of the 14th Regiment of Hussars which served in the Transvaal:

"Went up to a farmhouse where they were hiding. They opened fire on us at 1,000 yards and a bullet struck my horse Hoff. Fighting all day : got pom pommed while we were feeding. Routed the enemy and captured it when it was dark. Next day to Bloemfontain : got up and cut the railway. Buried our old and respected colonel, Col. Hon. Hugh Gough CB who lost his reason through overwork and shot himself."

"22 April on a flying column with General French and the Lancer's Brigade to Thabanchu, where we lost Captain Denny, shot dead through the heart, Sergeant Cunningham, hit by a pom pom and killed, Privates Pragnell and Amoore only lived a few hours and died of their wounds. I was lying beside a chap named Smith when he was hit in the neck and a lot of our squadron wounded including Corporal Spring shot through both legs and calf, Private Sheppard shot through both feet, Sergeant McQueen shot through the thigh, Sergeant Piper shot through the seat. We buried Captain Denny at the foot of the kopje with a Sergeant Soterton of the 17th Lancers. Return to Donkers Hoek where we heard of the death of a lot of my comrades from fever including 2922 Woods, Underhill, Hawkes, Akin, Hyde and Kenworthy. Private Watson was drowned at Mooi River." (15)

Despite dangers everywhere, so successful was Jack Kelly in his service with the Imperial Light Horse that he was promoted to Sergeant in the field. Such decisions were not taken lightly being a signal honour given the elite nature of the four hundred and forty man regiment and it was no doubt his strong personal qualities of leadership, rather than his style, that attracted the attention of his superiors. We can only guess at the attitude of his father - Jack was based in Lady Frere along with twenty thousand troops of General Bulwer.

As we have seen, in the early phases of the war the Boers had surrounded a number of towns with British populations such as Mafeking which lay deep in the Transvaal itself and Ladysmith to the east in Natal. The besieged Baden-Powell's reports from Mafeking reaching British Headquarters were desperate and from the perspective of public morale back in Britain something urgent had to be done. A flying column was therefore despatched from Lady Frere under the command of Lt. Colonel Plumer with the objective of breaking through Boer lines and relieving the town and Jack Kelly was a member of this column. On May 17th 1900 a column of troopers from the Imperial Light Horse rode proudly into Mafeking led by Major Karri Davis and close by was Jack Kelly - specially chosen for this mission along with an elite group of men from the Imperial Light Horse.

At 09.30 the next day a Reuters message arrived in London announcing that the siege of Mafeking was over and jubilant celebrations broke out all over London and the United Kingdom as at last there was something to celebrate. The war was however destined to last for another two long years during which time many more lives would be lost on all sides. On 8th January 1901 Jack

Sherwood Kelly was commissioned as a Lieutenant in the Imperial Light Horse - at last something of a great honour for Jack and his family. Unfortunately only five months later on 5th June 1901 Jack resigned his commission in a fit of temper and pique having had a major row with one of his superior officers. This was unfortunately not to be the last such incident and was a matter for the future.

In the end, the Boers were worn out and the peace negotiations that followed, led in part by Kitchener, resulted in the Treaty of Vereeniging signed in May 1902. For tens of thousands of men in uniform the war was thankfully over. For Jack Kelly this was a mixed blessing as the units of The Imperial Light Horse were one by one disbanded and he faced the question of what to do next.

(1)   'The Life and People of Lady Frere', an anonymous and undated
       pamphlet
(2)   Ditto
(3)   The Standard Encyclopaedia of South Africa, Volume 8, pp 632-636
       See 'The East London Daily Dispatch', 15th December 1874 and Lloyds
       Register of Shipping Losses, 1874-1875. See also 'Shipwrecks and
       Salvage in South Africa 1505 to the Present' by Malcom Turner.
       (C.Struik, Cape Town, 1988)
(4)   As recalled by Cmdr. A.J.Bateman, Norfolk, England
(5)   Emily Nuovo Abele Kelly. b. Queenstown, 18th May, 1878
       John Sherwood Kelly and Hurbert Henry Kelly b. Queenstown January
       1880
       Olive Rebecca Kelly b. Buffle Dorns, Cape Colony 10th April, 1881
       Edward Charles Kelly b. Buffle Dorns, Cape colony 28th November
       1882

Percy Dennis Kelly b. Lady Frere, Cape Colony 10th February, 1885

Gertrude Margaret Kelly b. Lady Frere, Cape Colony 5th April 1886

Oswald Claude Kelly b. Lady Frere, Cape Colony 5th October 1887

Clifford Terrance Kelly b. Lady Frere, Cape Colony 26th January 1889

Ethel Mary Kelly b. Lady Frere Cape Colony 26th December 1890

(6)   Dorothy Elizabeth b. Lady Frere April 1895

Henry James Collins b. Lady Frere July 1898

Patrick Dermott b. Lady Frere October 1901

(7)   St.Andrew's College Cadet Centenary Brochure, 1877-1977

(8)   From an article in 'The Daily Dispatch', (London S.A), 12.5.1989

(9)   Churchill W.S., p.19, 30 and 35-37

(10)   'The Nonqai' February, 1918. JSK Archives

(11)   For a more detailed survey of the role of Kitchener in The Boer war see:
        'Kitchener : Architect of Victory' by George H. Cassar. (Kimber)

(12)   'The Illustrated London News Record of the Transvaal war,
        1899-1900'. p.55

(13)   'The Original Despatches of Winston S. Churchill, War Correspondent
        1877-1900'. Ed. By F.Woods (Readers Union, 1975)

(14)   For a biography of the history of the ILH Website article from
        'The South African Military History Society'
        http://rapidttp.com/milhist/lhrcent.html

(15)   'The South African Military History Society Journal.' Vol. 10,
        No.6. The Diary of 3016 Pte. Horace Bell, 14th Regiment of Hussars
        http;//www.rapidttp.com/milhist/vol106hb.html

CHAPTER TWO

'There were some who thought he was too eager for fame,
and indeed the desire of glory is the last infirmity cast off
even by the wise'.
- Cornelius Tacitus AD 98

THE IMPERIAL ADVENTURE - PART TWO:
FINDING HIS WAY, 1902-1913

The general demobilisation ordered in 1902-03 of those thousands of men in South Africa left them with a long walk home. For a young man such as Jack, the war had taught many lessons not least of which was that there was an alternative to pointless study and the unreasonable discipline of the schoolroom. Indeed it is likely that the contrast between the discipline found in school compared very unfavourably with that found on the field of battle - not that Jack found either easy to deal with. Experience with The Cape Mounted Police had shown him that relative discipline combined with fear was a drug that appealed to him. Young men who challenge authority also know deep down that authority is necessary - it is all just a question of style and approach. Appeal in the right way and you have a devoted and courageous soldier but to get it wrong and worst of all be unjust and nothing would move him. Being made to feel subservient is one thing, being made to feel inferior is quite another and it was a lesson Jack had learnt the hard way.

A future with the British Army, if he could keep his temper, would no doubt have drawn Jack but this army was contracting not expanding. Even after their strong showing in the field, colonial troops were regarded as second or even third class troops and their officers similarly denigrated. Thus Jack Kelly's discarded field commission was in any event worthless in peacetime and effective only for the duration of hostilities. The old corruption of the purchasing of commissions may have ended in the English army with Cardwell's Army reforms of the 1870s but the patronage associated with it remained as strong as ever in colonial forces and entry into this precious club was not on merit but background and breeding - and as far as entry to the British officer class was concerned, Kelly had neither. Thus although by the age of twenty he could boast the British South Africa Company Medal for Service 1890-1897, The Queen's South Africa Medal and The King's South Africa Medal as well as mentions in despatches and a Field Commission, Jack Kelly was considered only fit for a Sergeant's rank when he decided to seize the opportunity to serve in an expedition to Somaliland rather than return home to Lady Frere.

Bounded as it is by The Gulf of Aden, Somaliland was a long way from the Transkei. The territory of Somaliland is a barren environment but its strategic position with The Indian Ocean to the south had often made it a site of interest to Imperial Powers keen to secure their route to India - this was especially so once the French opened the Suez Canal in 1869 linking The Mediterranean to the Red Sea. By the mid nineteenth century, Somaliland, with its Muslim culture seven hundred years old, was divided up between three of the great European Imperial Powers; France, Italy and of course Great Britain. This segregation of authority met with a response, for the revival of nationalism in the face of imperialism during the nineteenth century was not only associated with Ireland. The often immoral and illegitimate control by foreign powers could of course bring with it significant advantages in terms of social and economic development and stability, but it could also act as a catalyst for awakening dormant nationalist sympathies amongst the people. Thus the Italians had purged their country of Austrian dominance (and then set out to replicate that dominance on others), the Mexicans had removed the French and now Muhammed Abdile Hassan began his ride to death and glory in a campaign to rid Somaliland of the British. In a similar vein to his predecessor in The Sudan, the Mad Mahdi, Hassan set about torturing, burning and terrorising his way around the country. Very soon he also was awarded the title of 'Mad' by the British press and became The Mad Mullah - clearly any nationalist leader had to be mad in the eyes of the British press. The Mad Mullah of course represented a serious threat to British interests and finding him at the end of a British bayonet was the government objective. An expedition was ordered against him and a call went out in Africa for men to volunteer to support the regular force sent to Somaliland. We can only guess what motives drove Jack to take part but it was likely to have been a combination of patriotic desire to protect the Empire and the fact that he did not want to return home - it could also of course have been his quest for the Victoria Cross. Thus, out of the blue, another opportunity presented itself and Sergeant Jack Kelly, aged twenty-two made his way northwards across Africa to take part in another conflict supporting British colonisation specifically and the Empire in general. (1)

This time in the Burger Corps, Jack was again employed as a mounted infantryman and scout. Long distances had to be travelled to locate their quarry and the Mullah was adept at quick raids followed by equally rapid disappearing tricks which he put down to having supernatural powers. As was reported at the time:

"The notorious Mad Mullah who has been seeking to stir up rebellion in British Somaliland has fled across the border into Italian

territory and a British flying column has taken up the hunt accompanied by an Italian observer Count Lovatelli. The Mullah appeals to the credulity of the pastoral Somalis by telling them that he has supernatural powers. If they resist his demands then he returns with a raiding party to rob and kill. He then vanishes into the bush to lie low for months."

From his arrival in November 1902 to the end of the campaign in July 1903, Jack was involved in the tracking down of the Mullah. Again an article dated February 1918 in *'The Nongqai'* we have a reference to his being wounded whilst in Somaliland. The article was probably written from a selection of quotations about Jack popular at that time and we have no way of substantiating whether he was in fact wounded or not. (2) Eventually the rising was put down and Kelly was awarded yet another decoration - that of The Africa General Service Medal 1902-1904 with Somaliland clasp. However, as Jean Coulter also pointed out inevitably matters did not go smoothly and although he began as a Sergeant he returned to The Transkei as a private soldier. This was the result of another breakdown in personal discipline although it may not have been without good reason. As Jean Coulter and his great nephew pointed out, his demotion was as a result of "speaking out at his commanding officer." It really was becoming a feature of Jack's life either to challenge authority because he could not handle it or because of what he perceived as injustice.

It is tempting just to see Jack as an angry, temperamental young man totally ill-disciplined and determined to get into trouble and, despite his obvious personal bravery, doomed to self destruction. But there may have at times been good and laudable reasons why authority needed questioning - unfortunately the British Army was not the place to air them and this had already and was to continue to plague Jack Kelly's existence. His was to be a constant struggle with authority because he was prepared to question orders and challenge injustice, sometimes to the point of losing control. This was, in the eyes of the British officer class, especially intolerable from a member of the colonial units.

Loyalty to the Crown was felt very intensely in British imperial possessions around the world. The culture of the motherland, its values, attitudes, moral ambitions and history were fostered and developed into real and living forms by those transforming the empire into its own image. The books and poems of Rudyard Kipling, the music of Edward Elgar, the art of Landseer were all moving and emotional evocations of what people like Jack lived every day. Loyalty was perhaps strongest where it was most threatened and for people like Jack Kelly and his father, devotion to the British Empire and its way of life was a central feature of their lives. Now with the Somaliland expedition over, it was time for Jack to return home to Lady Frere and attempts to start a civilian life began - it was to be the only period in his life that he was out of uniform.

Jack did not want to return home. The new family his father had created was not close to him and there may have been a very strong resentment of his father dating back to 1894 when he had remarried so quickly. So, between 1904 and 1906 Jack was to be found working as a trader and recruiter of native labour serving the extensive mine works of the Cape and beyond. This was not to prevent his involvement in the crushing of the Zula Bambatta uprising in 1905-1906. This inclination or need to rush to any scene of conflict had become an established part of Jack's personality and character. It was something that would stay with him to the end of his life. There was something of the buccaneering spirit so deeply ingrained in his emotions that Jack was ever ready to drop what he was doing at any time and look for the next adventure on the horizon. It must have been hard therefore between 1906 and 1912 to have experienced a period of relative normality and stability as he continued to work in Butterworth alongside his younger brother Edward in the family labour trade. Even these six years could not remain uneventful and his life was rapidly becoming as turbulent as the turbulent times in which he lived.

Two events give us some flavour of life for Jack in South Africa at this time. Around 1910 Jack was giving some serious thought to the fortune and assets of one Emily Sarah Snodgrass. Recalling this period in Jack's life his stepbrother Henry James Collins (who died in 1983) remembered that, although able to show a romantic side, Jack was attracted to Emily for other reasons. Emily had been married before as is testified to by records in the Royal Norfolk Regimental Museum that state that "An ante-nuptual contract was signed between Emily Sarah Lawlor and Jack Sherwood Kelly on 15th May 1912." It is interesting to note that the 'pre nup' is not a new concept! We know that Emily was a widow when she met and was no doubt enthralled by the dashing Jack and they were married in early 1912. Marriage between a widow and a young man of thirty-two was not necessarily a problem but it was unusual given that Emily was in her forties. Edwardian social conventions frowned upon such situations as did Jack's father who wrote that "he should be ashamed of himself." This did of course not stop Jack marrying Emily but she was clearly astute enough to realise that she needed to protect her assets from the unpredictable as well as attractive Jack - and this proved to be far sighted as they were divorced soon after.

Whatever the benefits of marriage it seems that they were not enough to retain Jack's interest in sharing his life with another. Domestic bliss is not a phrase that comes easily to mind though without primary evidence it is difficult to assess with any degree of accuracy the exact causes of the rapid failure of the marriage. It is possible to speculate that his life to date had displayed considerable intolerance of others. He had moved as a free spirit up and down the ranks of the Empire's Armed Forces several times and coupled with his experiences at school one might assume that he was not prepared to compromise and that restrictions on his movements would be hard if not impossible to establish. Marriage to Jack was not an enterprise to be taken lightly - as later history demonstrates.

Prior to a court hearing in 1909 where Jack was due to give evidence in a local magistrate's court - not, surprisingly, as the defendant - Jack was found to be missing. A Constable was sent to look for him and he was discovered playing a tennis match which he had hoped to complete before running down the road to make his other court appearance. Having been summoned to report to the court of law Jack arrived complete with tennis whites, white shoes and racquet under his arm. The magistrate was by all accounts furious with this apparent disrespect for his court and ordered Jack Kelly to retire and return more appropriately dressed. Most people would have taken the hint and direction as it was meant but not Jack. As a local newspaper report described:

"The magistrate was too shocked to respond when the debonair young man returned to the court dressed in a full length morning coat, top hat and lavender coloured trousers. The final touches were given by the addition of his white gloves and walking cane."
(The Nonqai).

Flirting with danger and challenging authority, but with a sense of humour and keen to play to the crowd regardless of the consequences, tell us more about the man and his demeanour in his early thirties. Many would applaud the sentiment but lack the courage to commit the act, but while we can laugh and applaud we also have to realise that the limits beyond which he was prepared to go often plunged him towards the rocks of self destruction. Indeed this was also not going to be Jack's last appearance in court. Only ten years later in 1919 he would be attending his own court hearing, a Court Martial in central London, and one where he was antagonistic not only towards the entire British military establishment but also his nemesis Winston Spencer Churchill. Jack's brushes with authority and the establishment which he paradoxically fought to defend, had only just begun but would end in personal destruction.

At this point it is relevant to say something of the influence of Jack's younger brother Edward. Born on 28th November 1882, after the tragic death of Jack's twin brother Hurbert in 1893 at the tender age of thirteen, Edward became Jack's closest friend. Edward took his name from his grandfather who we may recall had fought in the Crimea. At his funeral in 1948 one Archdeacon Powell gave an oration which gives us a fleeting but meaningful insight into the character and personality of someone close to Jack:

"Edward Charles, or as we liked to call him 'Skipper' Kelly met his death as he and perhaps we ourselves , would like to meet it, without ceremony, without fuss, without pain. Death comes in many forms, but the form in which the door opens and shuts quickly is the best...so long as we are ready for the hereafter.

Skipper Kelly inherited a fighting legacy and he never dishonoured it. An ancestor of his took part in The Charge of Light Brigade; he himself joined Montmorency's Scouts when he was a mere schoolboy. He later joined Hartigan's Horse in World War Number One and was bitterly disappointed that an operation for appendicitis prevented him from seeing much of the fighting in German South West. But he was not to be denied and paying his own passage to England he joined the 10th Norfolk Regiment where he later commanded a company. And what a commander he was! He was severely wounded some six weeks after he was married in London and after the war he returned again to the Transkai transferring to Port Elizabeth in 1935. War disabilities hardened the hearts of the authorities and he settled down without uniform to do his civilian work ; he had been rejected but had the physical energy of half a dozen soldiers.

What underlay this somewhat blustering and impetuous exterior? A tremendous amount of chivalry and gentleness and real goodness. He was tough and yet gentle with a most charming chivalry to old people, especially poor people, perhaps his outstanding characteristic was his generosity : he never did anything by halves : he was a great giver."

Archdeacon Powell concluded:

"The Skipper loved his home, his life and children and his like we shall not easily meet again." (3)

Through these words can we discern an essence to be found in Jack. Impetuosity certainly has a resonance but so also do chivalry and toughness, however we cannot travel too far down this road in search of simple answers to a very complex man. What we do know is that both Edward and Jack were soon to be on the move again - the most momentous move of their lives as they set sail for Ireland in 1913 to fight in the civil war that seemed inevitable - another clarion call to arms which must have delighted Jack as he left South Africa behind for his next adventure.

(1)   Coulter Jean. 'East London Daily Dispatch', 12.5.1989

(2)   'The Nongqai', February 1918. JSK Archive

(3)   From the personal correspondence of Mr. J Kelly SA

CHAPTER THREE

'While war is terribly destructive, monstrously cruel, and horrible beyond expressions, it nevertheless causes the divine spark in men to glow, to kindle, and to burst into a living flame, and enables them to attain heights of devotion to duty, sheer heroism, and sublime unselfishness that in all probability they would never have reached in the prosecution of peaceful pursuits.'

Maj. Gen. John A Lejeune, 1929

IRELAND 1912-1913: THE ULSTER CRISIS AND THE ROAD TO WAR

In order to fully understand the elements of chance and circumstance which directed Jack and Edward to Europe in time to be caught up in the maelstrom of global conflict, it is necessary to be aware of a more parochial yet viciously intractable problem which had beset (and would continue to best) successive British governments - the so called Irish question.

Ireland and Irish nationalism had broken the careers of numerous politicians and even ended the lives of others yet all attempts at finding a lasting solution to the problem had, by 1910, failed. Like a rumbling volcano Irish affairs were always liable to explode in the faces of the most stable of British governments while for unstable governments the consequences could be catastrophic.

After his first appointment as Prime Minister in 1868 W. E. Gladstone had worked tirelessly to find an answer to the Irish question. His initial aims of pacifying the Irish failed as miserably as his later attempts at giving the Irish nationalists what they wanted

- Home Rule. It was over this issue that Gladstone not only gave up finally but split the Liberal Party irrevocably in the process. Gladstone's failure had in some ways highlighted the impasse that existed between the demands of nationalist passions in both the north and the south - the south wanting a united and independent Ireland and the north loyally determined to remain British. By 1910 the Irish question was reaching another explosive phase. Similar to the period between 1960 and 2000, sporadic and shocking violence produced a cycle that by 1910 had the British government in turmoil. The appointment of Sir Edward Carson as leader of the Ulster Unionists further increased tension and led to public pledges to protect the north and to retain strong links with Great Britain. Tension between republican and unionist factions grew and this time civil war was looming.

Edwardian England exhibited a new atmosphere of liberation and hope which contrasted sharply with the social control and weight of influence exerted by Queen Victoria and her key prime Minister Lord Salisbury which had reached its apogee in the 1890s. In his book on European history after 1880, J.M. Roberts characterises this period as one "…swept by gusts of sentiment and anger, unstable and insecure." (1) It certainly was a period of uncertainty and a crisis of identity for Great Britain. Increased communication, education, ambition and social change at home became mixed with a greater awareness of the vulnerability of Britain's place in the world, the pressures on maintaining the Empire and, closer to home, a real concern of the growing threat posed by Germany as she sought her "rightful place in the sun." This heady mix demanded flexibility and vision from government. It was a time where new problems needed new responses and approaches. To attempt to deal with these new tensions in the old ways was to court disaster.

It was against this backdrop that the lives of millions depended. The growing temperature of the Irish problem was also mirrored in our relations in Europe. The once enforceable and impregnable position of "Splendid Isolation" where Britain with its fleet and military reputation (encouraged since Waterloo in 1815 though harshly exposed in both The Crimean and Boer Wars as being a myth), was waning fast. The efforts of Edward VII to play a more leading role in European politics led him to closer ties with France (the entente cordiale in 1906) and with Russia through naval agreements and inevitably the combination of the two drove Germany further away. The performance of the British military in South Africa despite the colonial support of people such as Jack Kelly had at least resulted in the arrival of Lord Haldane at The War Office. With ten thousand British troops killed and a further sixteen thousand dead from disease whilst fighting an army of Dutch farmers in South Africa, Haldane's series of major military reforms were urgently required and went a long way towards creating an effective, well trained and motivated army that was at the disposal of ministers in the summer of 1914. The British Expeditionary Force may have been small and was largely slaughtered within months but it bought the time needed to create a new nationally recruited army to be led by Lord Kitchener.

To return however to the domestic problems that also beset this Edwardian government. The new Irish problem developing in 1912 -1913 should be seen against a background of problems piling up for Asquith who had succeeded to the leadership of the Liberal party in 1908. His predecessor's election victory in 1905 may have been a land slide victory against conservatism, giving Liberals three hundred and seventy-seven seats, but it was also marked by the establishment of radicalism in British politics. The new Labour Party (formerly the Labour Representation Committee or L.R.C.) had won twenty-nine seats and could no longer be ignored. Their voice was to be a loud one in the years ahead. However, the concern in some quarters over the growth of socialism was overshadowed by the various crises between 1909 and 1911. A series of related issues came together to create the crisis that was to bring Edward and Jack Kelly to London to fight for an 'Ulster that will fight and an Ulster that will be right.'

First came Lloyd George's budget. The financial requirements of funding both the massive legislation introduced by the Liberals and the cost of building more and more battleships in the arms race with the Kaiser meant the need for a radical budget which the Conservative dominated House of Lords chose to reject. This in turn led the Liberals to lean on the support of the Irish Nationalist MPs and they in their turn saw the price for this as new demands for independence from Britain at a point where Redmond, the leader of the Irish nationalist MPs in Parliament, was no longer interested in partial independence but wanted nothing less than a self governing and united Ireland.

In Ulster reaction was swift and calls went out for the creation of a volunteer force for the defence of the province should the British government surrender as they saw it in the face of Irish nationalist blackmail. A call went around the world for loyal patriotic unionists to return home to join a new paramilitary organisation. Civil war was now creeping closer and individuals such as Bonar Law, leader of the Unionist Party, fanned the flames declaring that "the unionists were the 'national party', the party of The South African War, the party of empire, the party of the assertion of British interests." (2) The call reached as far as Lady Frere in South Africa and sure enough both

Jack and his brother Edward answered. According to the memoirs of Henry Kelly, *'He (Jack) couldn't get there quickly enough - nor could Uncle Ted.'* (3)

Their enthusiasm was not of course out of character. Jack was thirty-three years of age in 1913 and had already fought in four conflicts in various parts of Africa. However, leaving their business to take up arms in the expected struggle in Ulster and sailing the thousands of miles needed to get there was new and a measure of the interest and commitment that they had to their homeland and their love for a fight.

Upon their arrival in Ulster both Jack and Edward would have been witness to the increasing tension and atmosphere of friction throughout Ireland. For two years, since its introduction into the House of Commons in April 1912, the Third Home Rule Bill attempted to make its difficult way through parliamentary procedure. To both sides, Asquith's position seemed to be one of vulnerability and he was mistrusted by both sides. Asquith had his own problems with trust. He had been warned more than once that the loyalty of the British Army, if called upon to act against The Ulster volunteers, should not be taken for granted. Indeed a number of British officers were in complete sympathy with the Unionist cause - they too believed in the defence of the Empire and its inhabitants. In March 1914, a cavalry brigadier general told the government that he and his officers would rather leave the army altogether than carry out orders to coerce the north. The Curragh Mutiny, as it has been recorded, was one of the last pieces in the drama that was unfolding in Northern Ireland leading, inexorably it seemed, towards civil war and no untold bloodshed. As fate would have it however, yet another nationalist cause had created major instability in Europe which was to overshadow all events in Ireland. Meanwhile Jack and Edward had arrived in Ulster and joined The Ulster Volunteer Force then forming up in Belfast and Jack Kelly was in uniform once more.

The assassination of the Archduke of Austria and his wife at Sarajevo on June 28th 1914 had sent a shock wave throughout continental Europe. This action ignited the frustrations, anger and fears of the Austro-Hungarian Empire and also provided a timely excuse to act for other nations who were so closely in competition with each other and so closely connected by the treaties and pacts signed in previous years.

What should have been a long hot summer break in England offering a respite from the many domestic issues instead turned into a frantic international political disaster. Events in Ireland took second place as the August Bank Holiday approached with the foreign ministries of the major powers working at fever pitch to contain what was now an international crisis. It soon became clear to Asquith and his Foreign Secretary Lord Grey that German support for Austria in her demands on Serbia had elevated this issue to a far higher and more dangerous level. By the last week of July 1914 Austrian troops were fighting in Serbia and Russian and French orders for full mobilisation had been issued. The Kaiser had pledged his support for Austria and a conflict with France seemed inevitable. If German troops passed through Belgium then this automatically brought Britain into the conflict as we had by the treaty of 1836 guaranteed Belgian neutrality.

In the main the loyal and trusting public knew nothing of these events. Throughout Britain the main thought was what to do with the sunshine. Farmers planned their harvest, fathers planned their family holiday and mothers planned their summer recipes. From Yarmouth in the east to Blackpool in the north and Folkestone in the south, thousands of people had arrived to enjoy what was one of the hottest summers on record. At the same time the newspapers carried increasingly disturbing reports of troop movements and the aggressive posture of the Kaiser.

The potential for war had a long pedigree and was not just the product of the assassination. It does not fall within the scope of this work to even try to explain the mass of conflicting aims, jealousies and intrigues in order to determine who or what was ultimately responsible for the slaughter that was to come. It is however necessary to examine a little more closely the political world which would determine the fate of millions.

In the final days and hours before the British declaration of war it is clear that Asquith and many of his closest advisors both inside and out of the cabinet had grave reservations about what needed to be done. Naturally the burden of taking the nation into war was far from straight forward but equally clear is the role that decisive and clear action can play in averting a crisis. In his book "Dreadnought" Robert Massie offers a most readable account of those final hours and concludes that "Asquith allowed events on the continent to outpace and influence decisions of the British government." This suggests a controlled and calculated indecision in terms of British involvement regardless of the military consequences in the short term. (4) But this was not a methodology confined to Asquith as his successor as Prime Minister, Lloyd George, was to employ a similar approach in events in north Russia later in 1919 - although that indecision was to be ruthlessly exposed to the British public by one Jack Sherwood Kelly.

Most people were well aware of the problems in Ireland and expected that, if there was going to be a conflict, this was where it would come. News that war was imminent in Europe came as a shock but one that became a reality when on August 1st Germany declared war on Russia. The die was cast when German troops moved into Luxembourg two days later on August 3rd. That same day Germany also declared war on France. The long overdue rematch threatened since the defeat of France by Prussia and the German states in 1871 was about to begin.

In Belfast Jack and Edward Kelly, like thousands of others, recognised that a greater cause was calling and both travelled on to a buzzing and confused London in late July. While ministers rushed around the corridors of Whitehall they were soon aware that events were passing them by. Even before the government had made up its mind to declare war on Germany, eight German Army Corps were moving across the Belgian borders as the Schlieffen Plan unfolded. In Britain tens of thousands of volunteers were queuing up to enlist in regiments in centres hastily being set up in church halls and schools. As German troops poured into Luxembourg and Belgium, thousands of people dressed in straw boaters and cloth caps waving Union Jacks gathered in Whitehall waiting for news and direction from the government. The excitement of war was everywhere, the mood was positive, the sun shone and confidence in the army and the navy was supreme.

Although Churchill, as First Sea Lord had already issued a stream of orders to the fleet and Haldane at The War Office had been sending out mobilisation papers calling back soldiers on leave and calling up reservists, Foreign Secretary Sir Edward Grey had as yet not made a statement to the House. He did so however just after 3.00pm on 3rd

August. He had walked to the House through the patriotic crowds milling and singing in Westminster and began his speech to a packed House. He began at 3.10 and one hour fifteen minutes later he concluded a rational and calculated speech detailing where Britain stood on an issue that was already out of control. Far too late, as many historians agree, Britain made its position clear. Britain had to act both in defence of its own interests, a moral obligation to France and a treaty obligation to Belgium - which by now had received an ultimatum from Germany to stand aside and allow its troops across its borders to invade France - movements that had in fact already been initiated. To paraphrase that excellent writer on this period Barbara Tuchman, Grey spoke to posterity whom he knew well would analyse his every move. Grey's words ensured that an ultimatum would now be sent to Berlin via our embassy but of course this was too late. It was delivered by the British Ambassador to Berlin Sir Edward Goschen but by 7.00pm on August 3rd 1914 - the next day Britain was at war with Germany. The roots of the conflict had been forgotten, the tensions between nations had not and the fuses had been lit all over Europe.

As a postscript to this briefest of summaries it is worth noting that one of the replies given to Sir Edward Grey in the House that day came from John Redmond who said:

"I say to the government that they may withdraw every one of their soldiers from Ireland. The coasts of Ireland will be defended by her armed sons...the armed nationalist Catholics in the south will be only too glad to join the armed Protestant Ulstermen in the north."

At two minutes past eight in the morning on August 4th 1914 the first waves of German troops in their field grey and pickelhaub helmets crossed the Belgian border and the British Army initiated their plan designed to meet such a threat.

The meticulous plans drawn up by General Sir Henry Wilson had been in existence for some time but Ministers now realised that it was time to read and understand them. Based on his observations, the availability of manpower and the known elements of the Schlieffen plan, Sir Henry had devised a scheme that was based upon putting a small Army of 6 Divisions into the field as soon as possible to form a block, much like a mobile brigade of today in Iraq or Afghanistan. The British Expeditionary Force as it was known was now hastily being assembled and famous regiments began forming up in camps all over southern England. Before it could move however:

"On August 5th, the first day of The Great War, the General Staff's plans, already worked out to the last detail by Henry Wilson, instead of going into action immediately like the Continental war plans, had to be approved first by The Committee of Imperial Defence. When the committee convened as a War Council at 4 o'clock that afternoon, it included the usual civilian as well as military leaders and one splendid colossus (Kitchener) taking his seat amongst them for the first time, who was both." (5)

From his position as the new Secretary For War, Field Marshal Lord Kitchener saw it as his duty to propound his deep apprehensions about placing the small but very well trained BEF in the hands of the French, holding the left of their line, and equally how they would fare against almost seventy German divisions heading for them. He feared that if this force was severely weakened or lost then there would be no time left to train the hundreds of thousands of volunteers that were now heading for the enlistment centres - they would be coming too late. His premonitions were echoed by Field Marshal Sir John French whose "mercurial temperament commonly associated with Irishmen and Cavalry soldiers" led him to believe that a sudden change of plan was essential to preserve the British force and give it an opportunity to make a real impact as opposed to being swept away in the tide of German field grey. On the opposite side was Sir Henry Wilson, his plan was on the table but time was vital and not on their side. To Sir Henry the council members were "mostly ignorant of their subjects" who "fell to discussing their subjects like idiots." His plan for the BEF had been worked out over many years down to a level of detail that any German staff officer would be proud, but the Germans were not controlled by committee. An alternative plan to land part or all of the BEF at Antwerp to save the port and advance to cut the German advance in two was put forward but it was at this point that Churchill stepped forward with a clear and unequivocal objection that the Navy could not guarantee a safe crossing for such a large force over that distance - Calais was far safer. And so it was that orders were issued for Wilson's plan to be put into operation immediately and the BEF began moving.

It is of interest and relevance to our story that only two months later Churchill, having initially dismissed the idea of using Antwerp, went on to implement the plan when it was far too late, despite many protests from senior officers. Churchill was always prepared to take risks with the lives of others to secure victory. This is probably a mark of leadership, making the important decisions is never easy and Churchill can never be accused of shirking the big decisions despite the cost. But often his decision making process could be described as reckless and needlessly cost many thousands of lives over his years in positions of authority.

The grand Schlieffen Plan had failed to encircle Paris and cut the allies off. The resulting stalemate saw the sacking of Von Moltke and the arrival of Von Falkenhayn who identified the siege now going on around the key post of Antwerp as a potential disaster to the advance. So did Churchill. Not having access to the Army, Churchill did however have access to the Marines and a force of 3,000 was sent to Antwerp to support the Belgians on his orders. So enthusiastic was Churchill that according to A.J.P. Taylor he even wanted to command the force himself. (6) As Robert Rhodes James pointed out, Churchill even offered to resign from his post at The Admiralty, which many would no doubt have loved to accept, and to take field command but was met with "roars of incredulous laughter". (7) How strange that two men could wish to sacrifice everything in order to rush to war - this determination of Churchill to lead his troops into battle was no different from Kelly deciding not to return home after the Boer War but to trek to the other end of Africa to fight in Somaliland. This was the soldier and cavalier spirit in Churchill trying to escape from the politician's body. In any event the attack was rushed and poorly planned and the brave marines ended up either dead or in German prison camps and the German attack swept on.

Given that Jack Kelly and Winston Churchill had already in fact served together in South Africa it was another twist of fate that their lives were now to become inextricably linked again for the next five years. The Antwerp fiasco, now forgotten as are many of Churchill's blunders have been in the tidal wave of the British need for heroes and victories despite failure, gives us a valuable insight into the character of Churchill as do the unmitigated disasters at Gallipoli in 1915, and also the rushed and ill thought out Narvik campaign in 1940. Both were failures and both were launched without proper planning and against the advice of many around him. In between these two disasters, in 1919, there was the Archangel Campaign - for a hundred years nearly forgotten. Here Jack Kelly would be instrumental in exposing Churchill and Churchill would be instrumental in almost destroying Jack Kelly.

In London the heady excitement and anticipation of war had now translated itself into a city at fever pitch. Excitement gripped the nation and everywhere recruits began swarming to local centres to sign up. Regimental recruiting teams began their exhausting work - not of persuasion but simply coping with the tidal wave of applications. It was in these early days that many under age young men saw their great chance for what they saw as excitement, glory and a chance to bloody the nose of the Kaiser and slipped through the fingers of hugely overworked recruiting officers and Sergeants. One such unit that was mobilised was King Edward's Horse in Central London. London saw recruiting dinners and parties, old officers came out of retirement, patriotic songs were written, newspapers inflamed passions, mothers said concerned and tearful goodbyes to sons, fathers shook hands with their heirs and pals walked arm in arm. Into this frenetic city Jack and his brother Edward arrived at Paddington Station in the heat of an August summer's day.

When Jack arrived in London on the train from Liverpool his world expanded before his eyes and ears. He had never seen a city of this size - this was the centre of the Empire. Buildings stood taller than the mountains of the Transkei and as he breathed the London air for the first time his lungs took in the air of a brave new world of opportunity. He arrived full of youthful energy, expectation and dreams. He expected much from London and was prepared to make whatever sacrifice was necessary to take it. His character by now was an aspiring one. He had left South Africa for one cause and now he had another - his own. The opportunity that London society could give him was immense and he knew it and his passport would be success in war. Perhaps here in England and specifically in London, Jack's restless spirit would find a home and a place where it could rest easy. Here he might be able to reach out and touch his destiny. Here all around him he saw colour, sound, people, energy and opportunity to make his name and fortune. There was little doubt that he was, as the King of Navarre exclaimed in *'Loves Labours Lost'*, *"stalking the elusive fame that all hunt after all their lives?"*

One of the main characteristics of Jack was his overpowering energy. We know that as a youth he was irrepressible and now he was simply stronger, larger than life and louder. He came into a room with a charismatic sense of certainty and confidence that enabled him to win over those around him, impressing them with his certainty and humour. But contemporary accounts also paint a picture of him similar to that of "The Skipper." In virtually every photograph we have of Jack we see a man in a state of calmness and certainty - a clinical look in his eyes. He knew himself and this was enough to lean on. Such traits were magnificent for leading men but ambivalent for those who were being led. Jack was instantaneous, dynamic, clear thinking and direct and he made decisions with ease and a self assurance that often unsettled or disabled his superiors. This speed of decision making also extended to his personality. He was quick witted and funny in company, his sense of fun and the absurd made him attractive in groups but he, as we know, was also quick to anger. In manner he was described as courteous to his inferiors - his soldiers adored him for his care and affection for them. To his equals he was magnanimous and respectful but to his superiors he could be rude, offensive and combustible - he had a problem with authority figures possibly ingrained from conflicts with his father. To be told to do anything was a problem for Jack - being told to do something with which he vehemently disagreed was an impossibility.

He was a man of magnetic charm, a refreshing and open contrast to the strict Edwardian codes that he stepped into. He was the life and soul of a social gathering and hugely attractive to men and women alike. He was not eccentric but he was extraordinary in his devotion to duty, to the cause of the righteous and the lengths he was prepared to go to protect the weak and challenge injustice. He was also attractively modest.

Extraordinary people often have an inner driver that sets them apart from simply the good and talented. Jack also had an abundance of energy - you do not fight in four wars by the age of thirty as a volunteer unless you have. Thus when he stepped from the train, the first people he met saw an ambitious, charming, tall and handsome man with intelligence and wit, a cavalier and evidently ready to make his mark and carry all those around with him. He knew his worth and wanted a stage on which to prove it so strongly that it would ultimately lead to his own self destruction.

As we have already seen in South Africa so also in the colonies of Canada, Australia and India, the mounted equivalent of the English Yeomanry Detachments were known as the Light Horse units. They were local formations formed for the defence of their homelands in support of often sparse police detachments. They were usually mounted and of course armed. In the majority of cases both the English Yeomanry and the colonial Light Horse units were led by leading members of the local aristocracy, gentleman farmers and squirearchy. Gentlemen farmers, landlords and their estate workers swelled the ranks of these part time units that existed in addition to the Territorial formations of the cities.

In 1901 Kind Edward VII had supported the raising of The Kings Overseas Dominions Regiment. By 1905 the regimental headquarters was based in London and consisted of four squadrons:
'A' Squadron - which was British Asian who wore an Elephant cap badge
'B' Squadron - Canadian with a beaver and scroll cap badge
'C' Squadron - Australian with a Kangaroo and fern cap badge
'D' Squadron - the South African with an Ostrich cap badge. (8)

The size and distribution of these squadrons varied enormously from country to country. However by 1909 'colony' squadrons were becoming associated with a past age and relations between Britain and the colonies becoming more sensitive and so individual squadrons were abolished and replaced by King Edward's Horse with unified cap badge composed of a shield with all the former squadron names embossed on a series of scrolls.

With the influx of volunteers arriving in London with colonial experience, a second echelon of the regiment (2/K.E.H.) was raised in London and, having made their enquiries as to where they could best serve in the new conflict, Jack and Edward Kelly enlisted in 2/KEH in the second week of August 1914. Thus the journey was now complete. Jack, who had left the British Army twelve years previously was now aged thirty-four and once more subject to the authority of the King.

By a strange quirk of fate, Jack's life was about to coincide of that of a young lady whose Irish origins and background were both markedly similar and yet also markedly different from his own.

Nellie Crawford Green's grandfather, William, a retired naval officer and landed Irish gentleman had in 1842 removed to New South Wales in Australia with his entire family and retinue. There he and after him his son George flourished. Indeed George became one of the foremost agricultural innovators of his age and helped to transform farming in Australia. His impressive granite house, Mount Oriel, completed in 1908, is testament both to his vision and his wealth.

When George died in 1911 it was no doubt his intention that his only son William should continue to administer his massive estate from Mount Oriel. William however was cut from different cloth, shaped by his Cambridge degree, education at Haileybury School and his experience as a yeomanry officer in King Edwards Light Horse in Australia. He determined that the family's future lay back in England and, the estate having been sold for a massive sum, it was there that the entire family, including his sister Nellie, relocated in 1912.

By 1914 the family had been permanently resident in England for two years. William and Nellie spent the majority of their time in fashionable parts of London - she had acquired a beautiful flat in Cranley Gardens in South Kensington and had a wide circle of friends. On the outbreak of war her brother William immediately volunteered for service and, given his previous rank, experience and social standing in London, was offered command of the 2nd King Edward's Light Horse with the rank of Lt. Colonel. Within days one of the first officers he met and invited to join the regiment was Jack Kelly and it was only a matter of time before Jack met Nellie and the circle was closed between the two families.

Thus is life. A chance meeting here, an event there. What some people call fate others call synchronicity. From two more differing backgrounds and two more different countries separated by tens of thousands of miles, Nellie and Jack should never have met. But despite its horrors, war creates as well as destroys. When Nellie first met Jack she was overwhelmed by his wit, charm, energy and huge self confidence. He was a Hercules, an embodiment of courage with compassion that melted her heart. Her brother could see it. Within days Jack was offered the rank of Lieutenant in KELH and being fitted out with the new officers uniforms. At the same time both Jack and Edward were integrated into the Crawford Greene's London social circle and there was no going back. Jack's new odyssey in the cradle of a landed and wealthy family with a war to fight had begun.

(1)   'Europe 1880-1945' by J.M.Roberts (Longman) p.143

(2)   'The Crisis of Imperialism' by Richard Shannon (Palladin 1984) p.406

(3)   From the personal correspondence of Mr J.Kelly in South Africa and also 'For valour : The History of South Africa's Victoria Cross Heroes' by Ian Uys. (Johannesburg 1973) p.261-265.

(4)   'Dreadnought' by Robert Massie. (Johnathan Cape, 1991) p.900

(5)   'August 1914' by Barbara Tuchman (Papermac 1987) p.96-97

(6)   Taylor A.J.P. "The First World War" Op cit p.35

(7)   Rhodes James, Robert "Churchill, A Study in Failure 1900-1939" (Weidenfeld, 1970) p.62-63

(8)   Information on King Edward's Horse is rare although a history was indeed published by Lt.Col Lionel James (Praed, 1921)

(9)   I am indebted to Rev Peter Long of Farnham who kindly researched and provided this information

60

CHAPTER FOUR

'Good relations between commanders and the rank and file are like all other forms of friendship - if they are to be maintained and bear fruit they must be nourished. Our men are exceedingly accurate judges of an officer's worth and character, and whilst they intensely dislike the officer who does not enter into their feelings and treats them as if they had none, they have unbounded admiration for the one who treats them kindly as well as justly.'
- Field Marshall Sir William Robertson, 1921

GALLIPOLI AND THE ODYSSEY, 1914-1916

While Jack was enjoying being smiled upon by Nellie and sharing her family's social entrée, the first phase of the Great War had come and gone with disastrous and bloody rapidity.

Initially the regular battalions of the British army largely went to France to be savaged in the early battles of the war as part of the BEF. The retreat from Mons, the Aisne and the Marne saw the flower of the army killed or wounded and it was only the stabilising onset of trench warfare that enabled Kitchener to build his new army. In the counties Service battalions were formed. These were still regular units but were in training, some were themselves broken up while others, when ready, were sent to France. Jack and Edward trained with King Edward's Horse between August and November 1914 before the unit was broken up and officers and men sent out to staff other regular battalions forming up in the Shires. In Jack's case he was promoted to full Lieutenant and commissioned into The Norfolk Regiment. Immediately on his arrival at the drill hall in Norwich it was clear that he not only had more active service experience than any other officer there but also more campaign medals and this, together with his evident confidence, led to his being promoted to Acting Major in The Norfolk Regiment. Already the war had dramatically changed Jack's life and far more was to come than he could possibly imagine.

As with most English counties on the outbreak of war, Norfolk had been broken up into districts for recruiting purposes. Peculiar to the agricultural way of life and of course temperament, the major job to be done was not fighting the Germans but bringing in the harvest. Once this had been done *"The Norfolk News"* proclaimed on September 5th 1914:

"..with the finish of the harvest, the Norfolk labourers were now rapidly making their way to the recruiting stations." (1)

We can only imagine the humour with which these lads, similar to young and old men across the nation, went home, packed their bags, said goodbye to their wives, children and mothers and said "well now let's see about this 'ere war". The harvest they had just collected was to be for many the last that they had gathered in during their lives. It was not the weather for war and the regular and reservist first troop trains were pulling away from loved ones in stations as early as August 6th. In places such as the market town of Attleborough however the harvest had to be gathered first. By the second week of August most of the able and fit men of the area were asked to assemble and take the train to Norwich to join the newly forming battalions - many of them never having travelled the fifteen miles to the county town - an adventure that would develop into a nightmare.

At the same time, the 1st battalion of their own county regiment had formed up, travelled to the south coast, crossed the Channel and by the 17th they were leaving for the front from Le Havre as part of 15 Infantry Brigade, 5th Division. By the 24th the men were already fighting for their lives with the Regiment falling back from Mons where it had engaged with the tide of German divisions flooding across the flat but scorched green fields of Flanders. Indeed on the 24th, two days after the Norfolk News proclaimed that the harvest was now in, the author's namesake was shot and wounded in the head, to die in Brighton a few days later, as one of the first British soldiers to die of wounds in England at the start of the Great War. Mrs Mary Matthews must have been one of the first Mothers in the country to receive a small brown telegram stamped 'War Office' which told her that her son Philip was seriously ill at a military hospital in Brighton. The war had already started to have an impact locally and she was the first of millions of mothers to suffer the effects - she was to receive two more such communications in 1916. (2)

In his 'Story of An Old Contemptible', Rob Kirk wrote about the head on clash between the best in the British Army and the best of the Imperial German Army - it was far from a Hollywood film but could easily have been where Private Forster was wounded:

"The foot soldiers (of the Norfolks) were deployed around noon, over half a mile of countryside between the mining village of Elouges and neighbouring Audregnies, among the slag heaps, rail lines, sunken roads and narrow cobbled streets of tiny terraced pit cottages. Tom Lawrence described it : "we were on a little ridge, Cheshires on our left, 119th on our right, and a clear field of fire across cornfields to the north west. Might have been back home in Norfolk!"

They were faced with the entire German VI Corps, outnumbered six to one in what has been called 'an extraordinary battle'. The horsemen of the Lancers and Dragoons charged but were beaten back, horses caught up in the wires and fences of allotments and tracks which criss crossed the countryside... Six thousand shells fell in two hours...the waves of field grey pressed forward...one German later recalled "they fired like devils, simply to move was to invite destruction...in our first attack we lost nearly a whole battalion." (3)

Heat stroke mixed with shell fire and blood, the British units were losing men all around and in danger of being enveloped and so the great retreat began...artillery batteries called for their horses and pulled back, infantry withdrew into streets and roads in good order but under heavy fire, runners taking orders were cut down and many did not receive the order to withdraw...

Back in England by the end of the month six thousand untrained but determined men had made it to Norwich and volunteered for service in the Norfolk Regiment - a colossal number for the time. The existing two regular and one Special Reserve battalions were now supplemented by the formation of the 4th, 5th and 6th Territorial Battalions (the Territorial Army having been one of the reforms created by Haldane). These part time troops now became full time and started making their way to the new training camps of Kitchener's "New Army" - which was designed and intended to win the war in 1915. With the arrival of this mass of new recruits a further four battalions of one thousand and two hundred men each were drawn up - the 7th, 8th, 9th and 10th Service Battalions.

To train and drill these new units was a real challenge. Most officers were either straight from Sandhurst or retired officers who last saw service in the Boer War. Their gallantry would not be in doubt but their ability to understand the new warfare that was emerging was. The tactics drilled into the recruits in the barracks on Mousehold Hill, like those for countless other battalions up and down the country, were to be stretched to the limit by the mud and machine guns and gas of northern France. For now there was still time for the drill Sergeants to turn boys into men and individuals into units.

One final unit to be mobilised at this time was The Suffolk and Norfolk Yeomanry. This was a militia unit based on similar lines to those of the colonial detachments of the Edwardian period. The Norfolk Yeomanry was led by a range of Norfolk landowners. Being virtually self supporting, they provided their own uniforms and tended to recruit their own estate workers as in days of old when retainers were the mainstay of the army. By 1914 the Norfolk Yeomanry boasted some four hundred men spread across four squadrons. Having said their goodbyes, the Norfolk Yeomanry was sent to form up in Woodbridge in Suffolk and it is here that Edward and Jack Kelly arrived to join their new unit which, on 7th February 1917, would be redesignated as the 12th (Norfolk Yeomanry) Battalion of the Norfolks. (4)

The winter of 1914-1915 was spent in various camps practicing sword drill, parade ground drill and fitness. However even as the trench lines and mass graves were spreading across Flanders there was still no call for the Yeomanry. These days of frustration to Jack must have been extremely hard but they gave him a chance to take the train into London Liverpool Street Station to meet with Nellie and enjoy dinners with his new found contacts and friends in London. Staying in London Clubs, Jack cut a dashing figure and of course he already had the swagger of an experienced soldier at war -

his perfect place in life. Dancing, the theatre and of course excitement characterised the early days as news of the reality of war was increasingly censored by the government now becoming aware of the nightmare that was unfolding in France. London must have seemed like a dream to Jack, replete in smart new uniform with a Major's crown on his sleeve, gloves and cane. While Jack was swaggering through parties and dinners in London and while Nellie was fast falling in love with the dash, confidence and smile of her new beau, Churchill was conceiving his plan for an attack on Turkey that would win the war.

With the Gallipoli episode the lives of Winston Churchill and Jack Sherwood Kelly once more come together - although neither realised it at the time. Almost as if they had been living parallel lives in alternative universes, both men had found school hard to cope with, were not naturally gifted academics, preferred the cut and thrust of excitement and challenge and revelled in being the maverick. Both men had gone on to volunteer for service in defence of the Empire - Kelly in South Africa and Somaliland and Churchill in Malakand and The Nile in 1898 and both cared less for praise and more for decisive action.

"The Gallipoli expedition was a terrible example of an ingenious strategic idea carried through after inadequate preparation with inadequate drive." (5)

Inevitably in war the lives of men were and still are used in experiments aimed at achieving victory. Against a backdrop of complex political and personal ambitions the soldier must fight, often for what he does not personally believe in. The Western front had, by the winter of 1914 - 1915, already taken shape as a killing ground on an industrial scale where reconnaissance showed no way through but offensives were launched anyway and ended where they had started. At the same time tens of thousands died proving what reconnaissance had already told them. The cost of speaking out against such futility was severe. For any Edwardian staff or general officer to question tactics or refuse an order not only meant immediate dismissal followed by Court Martial and very likely the death penalty (the first British soldier to be shot for cowardice was in August 1914) but also disgrace for his family and children. Jack Kelly, although not a typically Edwardian British Officer but an Irish South African with temperament to match, had as yet not arrived on the Western Front - if he had he would either have been killed quickly in some heroic but forgotten attack or rebelled and probably recoiled at the tactics employed by the General Staff. In this deadlock situation it was not the General Staff that came up with an alternative way to win the war in 1915 but the politicians - most notable of which was Churchill.

In his uncompromising style A.J.P. Taylor saw the Gallipoli campaign as having the potential to win the war if Asquith's government and the General Staff had the determination to see it through. But as history judged, it became a disastrous sideshow to the disastrous main event and saw the flower of the Australian and New Zealand Armies ripped to pieces by bullet and shell alongside their British allies and disease ravaged both.

Although Turkey was never part of the British Empire, consecutive British governments during the 19th century treated it as if it should have been. 'The Sick Man of Europe,' Turkey was always at the centre of some territorial or strategic design. Situated as it was between Russia and The Mediterranean, it represented a bastion against Russia and their entrance to The Mediterranean - depending on which side of the fence you were standing. To protect India and Africa the British navy did not want to face a Russian fleet sailing south out of the enormous pond of The Black Sea in The Mediterranean. When this looked probable wars broke out such as the Crimean War 1852-1855 where again thousands of lives were used to prevent the spread of Russian expansionism. When Disraeli purchased The Suez Canal Shares in 1875 Britain not only had a strategic interest in propping up the sick man but also a financial one. By 1914 Russian ambitions in Turkey had been replaced by German ones as Wilhelm II's imperial policy of Weltpolitik focussed on influencing and advising Turkey further, increasing tension across Europe.

The outbreak of war was not a surprise - even if the pace of events was. Prior to 1914 Churchill was to be found in the forefront of attempting to form a strong front against German imperial ambitions. He had after all been instrumental in supporting the naval arms' race. Although Churchill "broke down and cried" when seeing off Sir Henry Wilson and the BEF, Churchill presented a picture of "daemonic energy" in his expectations that Britain would defend Belgium. (6) His interventionist attitude was always very pronounced given that he favoured failure from action to the ignominy of inaction, and this was, as we have already indicated, demonstrated at great cost on numerous occasions. This was however a characteristic shared to a good extent by Jack Kelly even though it was Kelly who was to stand up and oppose one of Churchill's more delusional interventionist impulses in 1919.

Churchill had learnt nothing from Antwerp. As Gardiner wrote of Churchill:

"You may cast the horoscope of anyone else: his you cannot cast. You cannot cast it because his orbit is not governed by any known laws, but by attractions that deflect his path hither and thither. It may be the attraction of war and peace, of social reform or of a social order - whatever it is he will plunge into it with all the schoolboy intensity of his nature. His loves may be many, but they will always be the passion of a first love. Whatever shrine he worships at, he will be the most fervid of his prayers..."Keep your eye on Churchill" should be the watchword of these days. Remember he is a soldier first, last and always. He will write his name big on our future, let us take care he does not write it in blood." (7)*

Jack Kelly was just one of tens of thousands of men who became the instruments of not just Churchill's ideas but also those of the generals on both sides. In the case of Gallipoli the view of Churchill by Lucy Masterman captures the foundation of the campaign well:

"In nearly every case an idea enters his head from outside. It then rolls around the hollow of his brain, collecting strength like a snowball. Then after whirling winds of rhetoric, he becomes convinced that it is right; and denounces everyone who criticises it." (8)

Prior to 1914 significant efforts by the German foreign ministry had been aimed at drawing Enver Pasha, the leader of 'The Young Turks', into a reliance on German support against the British and Russians. Although Pasha had at one time been convinced that the future of Turkey depended on a strong relationship with Britain, in 1913 he cemented a relationship with Germany.

These political events did not fundamentally alter the European strategic situation as it existed either in 1914 or as it developed later. Turkey was not a first rate power. Indeed Turkey might have remained on the periphery had Britain not decided to prevent two warships being built in British shipyards for Turkey from being delivered. This simply pushed Turkey into the arms of Germany. On 26th September 1914 the Dardenelles were closed by the Turks, the entire length of the Bospherous was mined and the Turks hurried along with extensive fortifications to prevent any seaborne invasion. Despite this a seaborne invasion was exactly what the allies driven by Churchill attempted.

The inception of the idea has to be laid at the feet of Churchill. It was typically bold but also typically rash and if successful would quite possibly turn the entire war in France - if it failed then many thousands would die. Churchill however was not alone in believing that British troops could and should be used to better effect than "chewing barbed wire in Flanders."

Churchill saw that an attack on the Dardenelles was an appropriate strategy for a number of reasons. The devastating firepower of The Royal Navy could not be used in Flanders whereas it could be used to fire at Turkish positions. Secondly Russia was calling for supplies - these could be delivered via a tortuous route through the ice in the Baltic but far more easily through The Black Sea. Thirdly an attack on the Dardenelles would draw off German troops from the Western Front and lastly if successful the British and Commonwealth Army could drive into Germany from the south. Despite the problems and risks Churchill pressed on and as Lloyd George recalled:

"When Churchill has a scheme agitating in his powerful mind...he is indefatigable in pressing it upon the acceptance of everyone who matters in the decision." (9)

While Churchill worked through some of the details of a plan that he was convinced would end the war, the fate of thousands of men hung in the balance. In England divisions formed up and started to prepare for invasion from the sea while in Egypt the ANZACs, Australian and New Zealand Army Corps, were training in the dust and heat. Along the route to opening the assault Churchill was faced by a number of officers who voiced considerable doubt over the entire plan but Churchill overpowered each one converting their doubts into possibilities. His intense confidence and energy manoeuvred all objections out of his way:

"He always retained unswerving independence of thought. He approached a problem as he himself saw it and of all the men I have ever known he was the least liable to be swayed by the views of even his most intimate counsellors...unless the Prime Minister (as he was then) was himself impressed by the argument, pressure by others seldom had any effect." (10)

And even more telling:

"He was not easy to work for, particularly during the anxious days of the war. Patience was a virtue with which he was totally unfamiliar...his own rapidity of thought and expression was partly responsible for this, together with the fact that having been in a position to give orders all his life, and seldom obliged to execute them, he had no conception of the practical difficulties of communication and of the administrative arrangements." (11)

By the time the troopships set sail in March 1915 the Turks knew they were coming and all surprise had been lost. Naval bombardments continued into February and March but the serious damage to two British and one French battleship in uncharted minefields meant that the bombardments stopped and the Turks were alerted. Whereas this might have caused many commanders to reconsider it did not have such an effect on Churchill:

"I think I was pretty well trained to sit and manage a horse. This is one of the most important things in the world. Young men have often been ruined through owning horses or through backing horses but never through riding them - unless of course they break their necks, which, taken at a gallop, is a very good death to die."

Winston Churchill.

The men who landed into the horrors of Suvla Bay and elsewhere on that horrific coastline were making that gallop on Churchill's behalf.

The story of the Gallipoli landings of 1915 and the massacres that developed afterwards are well documented. Often Gallipoli is the poor relation of the Somme, Verdun and The Western Front generally - although not of course to the people of Australia and New Zealand. The months between April 1915 and January 1916 saw every kind of horror, miscalculation and disaster so typical of the battles in Flanders. The huge losses on the steep cliffs and small beaches selected by Hamilton crippled the attacks from the start and invasion rapidly became a fight for survival. By the end of June 1916 the key British formation, the 29th Division, had been severely mauled and thousands of its experienced troops had either been killed or were in hospitals throughout the Middle East. Instead of withdrawing, it was decided to press on with reinforcing the landings.

The Suvla Bay landings in August 1916 were as much of a disaster as their predecessors almost as if no intelligence material had reached Whitehall at all. Consequently one thousand men were killed on the first day and a further two thousand over the next two days as they tried to get off the beach. The strategic result was far removed from draining German manpower away from the western Front. Gallipoli was instead becoming a huge drain on allied forces. Quickly the Battalions that were being earmarked for The Western Front suddenly started planning for their war in Turkey. In addition individual officers were able to request a transfer and so it was that Acting Major Jack Kelly was transferred to Gallipoli.

The Spring of 1916 saw Jack and Edward Kelly continuing to train with the Yeomanry on the commons and fields of rural Norfolk and Suffolk whilst at the same time taking the train to London to meet with Nellie. However in June Jack approached his Commanding Officer and requested a transfer to help fill the many vacant roles in units in the 29th Division. Thus it was that Jack began his association with the 1st battalion The Kings Own Scottish Borderers who were part of 87th Brigade, 29th Division. The regimental diary of the KOSBs recorded by Captain Shaw carries the following entry:

"23rd July, 1915: A new Major has joined us."

The official battalion history carried on:

"The new major was a Herculean giant of Irish-South African origin, with a quite remarkable disregard for danger." (12)

Even from such a small piece of evidence it is possible to see that Jack cut an impressive figure. A large man with a large presence and a large temper, who within days of his arrival had already shown a reckless attitude to his own safety. Standing tall in a remarkable and rare photograph taken in the trenches at Gallipoli, Jack was indeed huge and like an oak with an officer's walking stick he dwarfs those around him. The wound stripes on his sleeve at the end of the Gallipoli campaign indicate that he was wounded at least and gassed twice. Jack perhaps saw life as the battle and the Turks as an opportunity - they were just another challenge to meet head on and another opportunity to fight - something ingrained in him since childhood.

During August and September Jack survived the merciless and dreadful fighting and as an Acting major would have commanded a company of over one hundred men of the 1st / KOSBs - a crack battalion from a crack regiment. Then tragedy struck the battalion as their history recorded:

"The old routine had hardly commenced when a dreadful calamity befell the KOSB. Their CO, and the orderly officer of the day 2nd Lt. J.D.Mill were killed on 15th October by the direct explosion of a shell from Asia."

Capt. Shaw had been half buried hard by one minute before and he described the gruesome sight that met his eyes, of limbs in parts of burned, bloodstained and shredded uniform and the eyes open in their sockets of men killed in an instant with no time to die or say their goodbyes. The in Commanding Officer was badly missed:

"He lived for the regiment, which was his sole thought: a strict martinet and very severe at times. Yet all respected him and most feared him too. Stoney was so tremendously energetic and strong, though a small, delicate featured, bronzed man, that we miss him exceedingly"

Captain Shaw.

"It may be added that he was a professional soldier and master of his profession. It was not only the hero of the landing and the disciplinarian, the calm, dignified, spick and span British officer, it was the man who knew the army machine in and out, who would see justice done to his officers, and who had a gift of clear exposition that was most missed." (13)

Between October and November Captain Cookson took command of the battalion and then word came through that Major Kelly was to take command of the whole battalion. For Jack Kelly this was a monumental challenge and we must recognise what had happened so fast. His rank of Major was only an acting one and only in recognition that he had previous service and that the Norfolk and Suffolk Yeomanry needed officers of a senior rank. Although he had been commissioned in the Boer War Jack had also been broken to the ranks more than once. Perhaps more importantly Jack had never been to Sandhurst to be trained as a British officer; he knew little of the expectations of the mess, old school ties and stiff upper lips; but he did know how to fight. To be catapulted into command of an elite Scottish battalion was either recognition of what he had already shown by his bravery and leadership skills or because there simply were not enough officers with experience around. Here at the stroke of a pen was rank as Acting Lt. Colonel, status, authority and responsibility - but it was not an easy fit.

"He (Kelly) had a gift for bombing, as for all branches of hand to hand combat."

Imagine the scene…a cold frosty morning in November 1915, Stand To ordered at 5.15 am, biting cold frosty winds with men's breath leaving their bodies for perhaps the last time…in front across the hard, frost covered ground, churned up by months of fighting the Turks only one hundred yards away, bayonets fixed, machine guns and handbombs primed ready for a rush assault to try to overwhelm the KOSBs positions... A Sergeant with muddy splattered helmet, worn out brown uniform and old woollen gloves and carrying his Lee Enfield rifle with a shiny eighteen inch cold steel bayonet fixed, walks along the wooden boards whispering in his broad Glaswegian accent under his breath, "stand still laddies, mark your target well, if they reach the trench give them the bayonet we're going nowhere get it "...."stand still laddies, mark your target well..." At the end of one trench on a corner stands a young Lieutenant, face blue on white with cold, green scarf from his mother around his neck, brown uniform with a single brass pip on the sleeve and a revolver whose metal is so cold he has to breath on it and hope it will fire when needed. His calves are wrapped in webbing up to his knee and his cloth peaked hat sat squarely on his head. He looks to his left at Lt Colonel Kelly, looking twice his size... huge man with a black moustache, square granite jaw and slightly double chin. No helmet for him just his red, black and while tartan forage cap to give a feeling of calm control...no fear in his eyes just an unblinking stare at the ground ahead of them. "B company present and stood to Saar!" Salutes the Sergeant. "Thank you, carry on" whispers the Colonel resting his cane on the sandbagged wall and taking his revolver from his large brown leather holster on his left hip. Looking at the young Lieutenant he mutters.. "Well, if they come now we had better be ready to give them hell..." He walks along the lines himself, having to stoop as his head and shoulders would show above the parapets, tapping and slapping men on the backs as he went, a team player, closer to the men than their previous CO whom they feared and respected, this CO made them wonder what he would do next...it was not unheard of for him to stand tall and shout "come on you bastards, have a go at us…we're ready for you"…quite unconventional for a Colonel in any regiment…not so much a stiff upper lip but rather a salty tongue. Not suitable for the barracks but in Gallipoli at Stand To it was ideal…

"His interest in ballistics extended to catapults, to obtain greater range. Such things would have been out of date on The Western Front, but on the Peninsula the catapult came into its own. The bold Major won the soubriquet of 'Bomb Kelly' and excelled in stunts on occasions alarming even his own side." (14)

Major 'Bomb' Kelly would reach for a pile of former tins of beef which were now packed with explosive and shell casings and a rough fuse through the base, light the fuse, the troops around him stood back, he stood up and holding a long stick in his left hand with a leather strap in his right would launch the home made bomb across the dead ground towards the Turks. Occasionally if he got his timing wrong, the tin would shoot off behind him or to the side and men scrambled for their lives as it went off - but it didn't half keep you on your toes. Often, when the tin hit the mark, out would jump Turkish soldiers to be shot by the KOSBs and up would go a cheer as the tin exploded. Much like a deadly game of cricket…The Major knew no fear and laughed & cheered if we got one right into their holes…

Jack Kelly therefore soon made a name for himself not just in the Battalion but throughout the regiment and right up to Divisional level. At one point Kelly was pulled out of the line by General de Lisle, CO of the 29th Division, to command the bombing school that had been set up as this was becoming the only way to kill the enemy at close range.

Adapting quickly to his new found rank and authority, Jack revelled in the role of Lt. Colonel and battalion commander- this was where he had always wanted to be. Never having had any training to command even a platoon of thirty men, let alone a company of one hundred and twenty or a battalion of over five hundred, he reacted as if he had been born to command - but in his own way. Thus the Herculean Colonel, while popular with the men of the KOSBs who saw him as a team man, closer to them than they had ever felt any officer, found relations with his fellow officers more difficult. This was what was noted in the regimental diary as a "change in mood and method."

Despite the careful phraseology of the regimental history we can easily see and understand that Kelly was not part of the normal officer machine - this disjunction would ultimately lead to a clash of monumental proportions in 1919 and the seeds were being sown now on the muddy, blood stained slopes of Gallipoli. Kelly had been trained in the field of life in South Africa not the playing fields either of Eton or Camberley. He fought as he thought and not how he was taught. At times this may have saved the lives of many of his men but possibly cost lives at other times. Breaking with the expected or traditional was not deliberate it was natural for Kelly, almost like a law of nature. Even though a Scottish Regiment through and through, it was like most Scottish Regiments led almost exclusively by English officers as such regiments had always been. Clearly Kelly was respected for his bravery, courage and impressive physical stature but he was held on sufferance by his fellow officers. He had risen to his rank through chance and good fortune, kick started no doubt by his relationship with William Pomeroy Crawford Greene back in London a few months before - and by the death of the former CO. What could have taken fifteen years of hard work as a career officer and a good deal of other necessary attributes such as having gone to public school and University had been achieved by Kelly after expulsion from his and with no experience of Oxford or Cambridge, save meeting there for dinner with Nellie. All of this he could have survived but for his colonial background which was looked down upon, marking Jack as a necessary evil serving a useful purpose. Given the heavy and increasingly desperate losses he was also good for the morale of the fighting men who saw him as something of a talisman. Delicately worded in the regimental history we find the phrase:

'It may be added that he was what is called in Scotland a 'character' and possessed a strikingly vigorous if not specially wealthy vocabulary.'

How wonderfully and typically British, such understatement which we can see though to really mean in current parlance he swore a great deal and was almost uncontrollable and mercurial in temperament and to the devil with the consequences.

This was followed by:

'It (the withdrawal from Gallipoli) was soon accomplished and the KOSB maintained their reputation throughout the Kelly interregnum'.

We could read that in so many ways and that no doubt is how it was meant to read. The official history probably seeks to say that despite the Kelly period they were able to preserve their reputation of a British regiment still able to fight and die by the textbook that was proving so utterly useless on The Western Front. It was better to fight and die within the rule book than to challenge authority and do it another way. Yet that at his heart was Jack Sherwood Kelly. Not just hard headed, stubborn and offensive at times, but also courageous enough to try another route and if necessary speak out and challenge - not talents required or expected. He was at odds with a system of authority that had already shown him what it expected. It needed him but not what came with him. A system that wanted to win the war but in its own way and in its own time. Churchill, had he been in Gallipoli even for a day would undoubtedly have been at one with Kelly and his adventurer spirit. But he was not.

As November progressed into December 1915 the weather worsened and the cold hit well below freezing. In his "Gallipoli Diary" Major John Gillam DSO described just one night in the trenches of Gallipoli:

"Last night the frost was severe and the men lying out in the mud behind the soaking trenches suffered the greatest hardship that a soldier could endure - namely lying in soaking clothes, which freeze stiff in a biting wind, while the temperature falls to below zero.

In front of the 86th Brigade the Turks hold higher ground than we do and I think that they must have opened one or two of their sapheads when their trenches were flooded, thus allowing their water to rush over to our side engulfing all our first line dugouts and communication trenches. Officers in the line, if they were not on watch, were huddled together all night endeavouring to get warmth from each others bodies. Telephone communication broke down and many men, cut off from the rest and having to watch the enemy, froze and died at their posts overnight."(15)

Back in London discussions had been going on for weeks about whether and how to withdraw from this disaster. In Gallipoli however:

"The KOSB might have had a quiet time in the trenches but Col Kelly was in his element nursing the fighting spirit and entries in the War Diary show that on the 9th and 10th November continuous catapult bombing day and night seriously damaged the parapet of a Turkish trench." (16)

Whereas many would hope to lay low and survive not angering the enemy, Lt. Col. Jack Kelly was just at it the whole time aggressively taking the war single handed to the whole Turkish Army. This did not come without cost and on 21st October 1915 Jacks lungs were badly burnt by a waft of gas sent over from the Turkish lines. He was moved to hospital on the beach the next day but was so badly burnt that he remained there until 28th October when he then volunteered to return to the front lines even though he could have taken a troopship home. From then on breathing was more difficult for him for the rest of his life. (17) His shoulders were often hunched over trying to compensate for the harshness of breath that he felt especially in cold weather. Jack was also wounded by shrapnel in his left shoulder although not badly enough for him to leave command of the battalion he was so proud to lead.

The exploits that marked Kelly's period as CO of the 1st battalion should not have been unexpected. He had landed but a few days the previous June and had already made his mark leading a frontal attack across to Turkish lines. This was no doubt where his reputation for courage came from. According to Ian Uys, and despite being wounded at least three times, Kelly led from the front, pressing home an attack from which only six men returned. There is some evidence for this as his Gallipoli photograph clearly shows three wound stripes on his cuff that could only have been awarded in Gallipoli within the six month period that he was there. (18)

At Brigade Headquarters there was a need for good and stirring news and what better than the latest escapade of Major Kelly the mad South African. Jack was recommended for the award of the Distinguished Service Order and the necessary papers were dispatched to go through the formal channels. Meanwhile the decision had been taken to withdraw, rather than retreat, from Gallipoli.

A while before the decision was taken the barrel of men was running dry. All over the slopes, cliffs and beaches at Gallipoli men lived in the earth, baked in the sun by day and frozen in the cold of each night. Poorly provisioned and constantly bombed, disease ran unchecked among their numbers killing as many men as the Turks. The ANZAC's suffered terribly and into this hell the Norfolk and the Suffolk Yeomanry were ordered in September 1915. With only weeks to go before the order to withdraw was given, the Yeomanry were at last ordered from their camps in East Anglia to make for Southampton to board the SS Olympic - sister ship of The Titanic. What a cruise that must have been - ten days on board the world's most luxurious liner. Passing through the Straits of Gibraltar and on into the Mediterranean, it must have felt like a journey to the other side of the world for these lads and their officers for whom a walk to Norwich was the highlight of the year. They were typical of their type - largely estate workers such as The Sandringham Company because all the boys worked on the estate and their officers were the senior clerks, managers, surveyors and gardeners of the royal estate in North Norfolk. The Suffolk Yeomanry was even more like a company of retainers from the Middle Ages following their knights into battle. They boasted in their battalion alone twelve existing and former members of Parliament and, in case there was time to chase the Turks on horse back, twenty-two former masters of Fox Hounds! What was certain, although they did not know it as they watched the waves crash around the enormous sides of this huge ship, was that whatever they had learnt waiting for their chance to fight, it was going to be of no use at all as they stepped onto the carnage and pain of the Peninsula.

The eight day journey ended with the sound of gunfire and smoke ahead of the ship. Setting anchor in Mudros bay on the island of Lemnos, they disembarked with shiny boots, polished leather and oiled rifles into small ferries and landed in Suvla bay on 10th October. They never got off the bridgehead. Pounded by artillery as they landed, there was nowhere for them to go save replacing men on the bridgehead who were being taken back on the same boats that they had just left. Under the command of 54th East Anglian Division, they would have recognised broad Norfolk accents all around them. Men from the same villages would have recognised each other, exchanged news from home and swore about the Turks and wondered what the hell they were doing here when it was the Germans that they had gone to war with.

Implicitly trusting in their officers, men whom they had worked with all their lives, they did what they were asked to do. Within a week seventeen other ranks had been disembarked with dysentery and within a month this number had grown to one hundred and thirty-nine - only one man had been killed by enemy fire. The sewage and stench of death with so many men using the same facilities and such extremes of cold were being killed without a fight. By November 27th, where further inland Lt.Col. Kelly of their number was bombing the Turks by hand, they had lost one hundred and eighty-nine of their troops to disease. Had Churchill been there to see for himself what power he wielded he might have thought twice before embarking upon such a scheme again.

"It so happened that on the 12th November that when I was buying wine at 'The Intendence' at Sedd-el-Bahr (Egypt), I saw a small group of French and British officers of distinction saluting a tall man who had just embarked in a boat. That's very like Kitchener I thought, and dismissed the subject from my mind. Sure enough it was Kitchener, and his visit had momentous consequences." (19)

Having taken the decision to withdraw, the crucial question was how to get out without losing the entire army to a Turkish slaughter. Much has been written about the ingenious deceptions that were carried out starting in December 1915 and January 1916, so much so that in that peculiarly British way a total disaster was transformed into a great victory - but the casualty figures spoke for themselves. The number of killed and wounded was estimated at one hundred and seventeen thousand along with a further one hundred thousand evacuated with dysentery and other diseases - of which fifty thousand died. The horrific statistics of the Somme should not be allowed to overshadow the suffering that took place at Gallipoli.

As for Jack his temporary command as Lt. Col came to abrupt end. During December the Yeomanry was being evacuated from Gallipoli and according to their regimental history A/Major Kelly arrived back to the Norfolks to aid them with their withdrawal. They had not engaged the enemy as they had hoped and some of their comrades had been lost - as one New Zealander put it "*it was not our wasted energy and sweat that grieved us. In our hearts it was to know we were leaving our dead comrades behind.*"

(1)   See Mansfield N. "Volunteers and Recruiting" from 'Norfolk & Suffolk in the Great War' (Gliddon Books, 1988)

(2)   See Bujak P 'Attleborough - The Evolution of a Town' (Poppyland Publishing 1990)

(3)   "The Devils Orchestra - The Story of an Old Contemptible". By Rob Kirk, 1997

(4)   For more information on The Norfolk Yeomanry see "The Norfolk Yeomanry in Peace & War 1782-1961" by J. Bastin (The Iceni Press). According to Col. John Boag OBE, MC, TD DL, the Norfolk Yeomanry kept few documentary records during The Great War. Those that do exist are currently held in The Muckleborough Collection in north Norfolk

(5)   Taylor A.J.P. "The First World War". (Penguin, 1963). pp.80-81

(6)   Tuchman 'August 1914', Op.Cit. p.97 & 205

(7)   Gardiner "Pillars of Society", pp.61-63

(8)   Charles F.G.Masterman in "CFG Masterman", by Lucy Masterman. (Nicholas & Watson 1939). p.26

(9)   Lloyd George "War Memoirs" Vol.I, p.395

(10)   Colville, John. "The Fringes of Power, Downing Street Diaries 1939-1955". (Hodder & Stoughton, 1985). p.125

(11)   Ibid p.126

(12)   Regimental History 1/Battalion The Kings Own Scottish Borderers' Ch.VII, p.166 dated September - October, 1915

(13)   Ibid p.166-167

(14)   Ibid p.167

(15)   'Gallipoli Diary' by Major John Gillam DSO. (The strong Oak Press, 1989), p.267

(16)   Ibid p.168

(17)   See letter from Jack dated 26.2.1916 to The War Office requesting pension rights for his wounds in Gallipoli - National Archives, Kew

(18)   Uys, Ian 'For valour : The History of South Africa's Victoria Cross Heroes'. (Johannesburg, 1973). pp.261-265

(19)   KOSB's Diary p.169

CHAPTER FIVE

Questioned as to how he had gained his great reputation, he said,
"By having despised death."
- Plutarch, quoting Agesilaus, Eurypontid, King of Sparta
(400-360 BC)

THE SOMME, 1916 AND MARRIAGE

By January 1916, both the Norfolk Yeomanry and The 1st Battalion of the King's Own Scottish Borderers were recovering in Egypt. The whole of 29th Division had been withdrawn to Egypt and, leaving thousands of their friends and comrades in the sands of Gallipoli, the men were dazed, tired and shocked. Whilst the Norfolks were then soon on their way home, the KOSBs were kept near the Suez Canal "where it remained for two months, training and guarding the Suez Canal."

At the end of January Jack returned to England with The Norfolks. Landing at Portsmouth at 5am on a cold and freezing English morning, he then took an early train for London. Before he left he sent a telegram to Nellie letting her know that he was alive and well and when he would be stepping from the train. His gas wounds were playing up though and his bones were bruised from the two wounds he had received so the cold January air made for a hard few months ahead.

Arriving back at Waterloo Station must have been a quite surreal experience. Virtually every day there were military bands sitting in corners which struck up whenever a train arrived or fresh units left for the front. The steam and smoke billowing up high into the cold black steel roof together with the noise of train whistles surrounded his ears as he stepped onto the platform, people everywhere - some with the look of innocence as if there was no war at all - others with their eyes carrying the reflections of death that they had witnessed. On this day Nellie was there to welcome him. Standing on the end of the platform she looked a wonderful sight of feminine charm, beauty and high fashion. Her neck surrounded by a light brown fox fur collar and her head sporting a warm fur hat, Nellie smiled a beaming smile as Jack advanced in full glory down the station stick in hand but also with a huge smile beaming from his broad mouth and his chest like a barrel full of rum.

While Jack had been waging his own personal war in Gallipoli, he had also been conducting a campaign to gain the hand of Nellie in marriage. She had fallen completely in love with the proud, dashing, confident Jack when they had first met in the July of 1914 - since then she had been haunted by the thought of Jack being ripped away from her and being killed. But on this day she had him back. On leave for the next two months to recover from his wounds, Jack arrived in London with a uniform already displaying an impressive array of decorations, the insignia of a Lt. Col. and the wound stripes of a man who had already seen action at the front. Such was the meteoric change in fortunes and indeed direction and purpose that two years of war had brought to Jack's life. Conflict brought the best out of him and he performed like a star in a new play on the West End. He walked and swaggered as a natural hero should and never looked back at the risks that he had run - overstepping the mark was always just around the corner. Nellie on the other hand was the essence of respectable and wealthy London society. Gentle and calm, she was the sunshine in the morning after Jack's rainy thunderstorm in the early hours.

One of the many quirks of fate that have affected the research for this book is that as I write this chapter I can almost see the home where Nellie and Jack Kelly lived. This means that as I walk the streets on a normal day I can imagine around me the buildings that they both would have seen on their journeys around town. At her home at 21 Cranley Gardens Nellie had a circle of well connected and wealthy friends that her new beau could easily fit into. He was the picture of heroic and strong manhood that everyone wanted to see and associate with. Jack's military image worked well with Nellie's wide and fashionable socialite position in London and to everyone who knew them it seemed the ideal match. The 2nd of February 1916 merely added to his status in London circles when the War Office sections of the London Gazette announced the award of the Distinguished Service Order as a result of his actions the previous summer. At the start of the war it was normal for the newspapers to carry detailed accounts of the acts of bravery performed by British troops in receipt of awards for gallantry. However by the Spring of 1916 so many medals were being awarded that this practice had waned in all but the most spectacular of circumstances. The standard work on the DSO is that by O'Moore Creagh which carried a simple notation of the award stating that, at the time, Jack was still on the strength of the Norfolk Regiment. It was The East London Daily Despatch that carried the first recognition of Jack Kelly serving with the British Army - it was to become a regular relationship with the press over the next few years.

...it was the Major's fine leadership, coupled with remarkable personal bravery - to which there is ample personal testimony - that won him the DSO...such has been his efficient work and steady perseverance.... (1)

The previous October another article had appeared this time in a newspaper in South Africa. It had been written by Mr Bernard Oppenheimer who announced that he would give £100 to each of the first South African recipients of the Victoria Cross and £50 to the first ten winners of the DSO. Come January 1916 Mr Oppenheimer was already out of pocket but the first to receive his medal was Lt. Col. Jack Sherwood Kelly. On hearing of his gift Jack immediately announced that he would donate his prize to The Frontier Hospital at Queenstown - where his mother had been taken back in 1892. The news of this act of generosity was not lost on Mr Oppenheimer who again wrote:

"Dear Sir,
Having heard that Lt. Col. Sherwood Kelly learned about my recent offer from 'The African World' whilst on active service in Gallipoli - where he won the DSO for conspicuous gallantry - and that he desires to send the amount to the hospital at Queenstown, his native town in South Africa, it gives me great pleasure to inform you that I have despatched the amount of £50 to the secretary of the Queenstown Hospital by this weeks mail with the best wishes of this gallant officer."

The British press began to take more of an interest in Jack's career and Reuter cables carried news of his donation and that he was "greatly admired" by the Queenstown community.

Throughout March and April 1916 therefore, Jack was able to relax into London society, a world of parties for the war effort but also growing confidence in the big push that would see Kitchener's New Army Divisions bring the Germans to heel - 1916 was to be the year of victory. Such confidence may have contributed to the blossoming romance between Jack and Nellie - we can imagine evening dinners, flowers, walks in Hyde Park or along The Strand and eventually a proposal of marriage from Jack - which was accepted. All the while in the background the detailed planning of The Somme offensive scheduled to begin in June or July 1916 was going on but for Jack and Nellie such things could wait and be put to the back of their minds as a whirlwind marriage was planned before Jack was posted to France. They made a wonderfully romantic pair - Jack with his impulsively strong and confident air, his laughter and devil may care sense of bravery, a row of medal ribbons that would put many an officer senior to him to shame and wound stripes to show he had already seen serious action and survived. Nellie on the other hand is best described by an article written about her in The Ladies Field in February 1916 where she was described as "…a pretty graceful woman of literary and artistic tastes." (2)

The photograph that accompanied this description reinforces these comments in spades - a tall but gentle posture, small long hands held elegantly in front of her fashionable Edwardian dress. Jack in the same article cut the posture of the Cavalier, the sword replaced by a walking stick and breastplate replaced by a strictly ironed uniform resplendent with brass collar dogs and medal ribbons that now included the DSO. His sparkling if unconventional military career to date was now overlaid by the aura of a hero. He was still likely to fall foul of the establishment whether it was a general or the manager of a restaurant but this was now seen as part of what heroes did rather than being the hallmarks of a bad tempered and angry man.

Living as she did in still fashionable Cranley Gardens, Nellie chose to get married at St Peter's Church. Having been closed in 1972, St Peter's is now The Armenian Church and it stands less than 50 yards from Nellie's home and we can imagine that bride and groom left at slightly different times to walk out of their front door to the right and 30 seconds later into church - at least the reception would not be too far away. St Peter's today is still very much a pretty and ornate but small church nestling as it does within the imposing family residences around it. According to the marriage certificate, Jack was not resident in London but resided at Margery Hall in Reigate in Surrey. He had by all accounts an aunt - a patriotic woman of some means who let Lt. Col. Kelly a flat and he could then catch the train into town very easily. So it was that the marriage took place on April 22nd 1916. There is no pictorial evidence of the event but it is likely to have made quite a sight with members of Nellie's wealthy family mixing no doubt with some of Jack's fellow officers from the Norfolks - we do not know whether fellow officers from the KOSBs attended. However, it is in the detail of the marriage certificate that we again uncover something of the man and the event.

One of the witnesses to the marriage was E.E. Greene. This was Nellie Elizabeth's mother. However her brother was not a witnesses and had he not been serving in Palestine he almost certainly would have been. The other witness' were H.G. Evelyn Vardon and Julia Wilson. Perhaps Elizabeth's sister Georgina was also there. The certificate also records that Jack described himself as Lt. Col. 1st Battalion KOSBs which indicates that although he had left Gallipoli with the Yeomanry, he was still listed on the strength of the KOSBs. Under 'condition' Jack described himself as bachelor which indeed he was - although for the second time as we know. However most interesting of all is that Jack lied about his age. Having been born in 1880 he was clearly aged thirty-six in 1916, however he listed himself as aged forty-two. This can only have been to narrow the gap between himself and Nellie who was aged forty-four and marrying her dashing young, but already emotionally charged and scarred young officer.

We know nothing of the honeymoon or how long it lasted but it was quickly brought to an end. The war was never far away and the four month period between January and April 1916 was merely an interlude of calm between two storms. To the far south in France the Germans and French were slaughtering each other at Verdun. As the German's attempted to 'bleed the French Army white' so the French under Petain were saying 'they shall not pass.' The officers and men on both sides who fought for these battle cries went through a hell and horror hitherto unknown in history as the mountains of skulls stored in vast ossuaries at Verdun today testify. Meanwhile in Britain life went on as normal. The government was harangued daily about their general strategy and the socialist threat continued to grow. Shortages were becoming severe and supplies from overseas were increasingly threatened by submarine attack. Thus the pressure on Field Marshall Alexander Haig to strike a blow, so hard that the war would end, mounted daily. In response he prepared his Somme offensive and in early May Lt Col Kelly was ordered back to the front having only spent a matter of days with his new wife. The Regimental Diary records:

'On 19th May Lt. Col A.J.Welch, just a year and seventeen days since his wound, resumed command... Lt. Col. Kelly was given another command in the division.' (3)

This new command was to be as C.O. of the 1st Battalion of the Royal Inniskilling Fusiliers. From the outset we must conclude that whatever his reputation for not being popular with his fellow regular officers in the KOSBs, Kelly must have been regarded as a strong front line officer. Not only was he young and already highly decorated but he was commanding a front line regular battalion - all the early numbered battalions (1, 2, 3 etc) were the best that the regiment could muster. He may have been given command of 1/KOSBs due to the huge losses in Gallipoli and the need for experienced officers but in Kitcheners new army this would not have been the case. His appointment to command another 1st Battalion was on merit and reputation.

Moving from a Scottish to a largely Irish regiment also made sense - at least he could share the same jokes, language and temperament and argue with whom he liked - like most Ulstermen if there was not an argument going on he would create one. On the strength of the 1/Inniskillings Kelly was still listed as being on attachment from the Norfolks and the regiment would have been proud of this career to date. One can imagine the interest and excitement as the new Colonel arrived to take command and the sense of fun and determination that Jack brought with him as he arrived back where he belonged and possibly felt most at home - in a war. The Inniskillings had a long and proud fighting history that covered battles at Badajoz in The Peninsular War, Waterloo and many others. The regiment had been formed in 1881 and had grown to twelve battalions during The Great War and was to earn eight Victoria Crosses.

During May and June 1916 the build up for the Somme offensive continued. The 29th Division, which had arrived from Egypt in Marseilles on 29th March and marched to the Western Front, formed up in three Brigades each commanded by a Brigadier and each of four battalions commanded by a Lt. Col.:

86th Brigade: 2/Royal Fusiliers, 1/ Lancashire Fusiliers,
                16/ Middlesex and 1/Royal Dublin Fusiliers.

87th Brigade: 2/South Wales Borderers, 1/KOSBs,
                1/Royal Inniskilling Fusiliers, 1/Border Regiment.

88th Brigade: 4/Worcestershire, 1/Essex, 2/Hampshires,
                Royal Newfoundland Regiment.

(4)

All in all therefore the 29th Division was a strong and experienced division with some highly trained and professional high number battalions and it formed up as a key part of the line. To illustrate the point and to help understand the slaughter that was to soon follow one can look at the 24th Division which again was composed of three brigades:

17th Brigade: 1/Royal Fusiliers, 3/Rifle Brigade, 8/Buffs and
                12/Royal Fusiliers.

72nd Brigade: 1/North Staffs, 8/Queens Royal West Surrey,
                9/East Surrey and 8/Queens Own Royal west Kent.

73rd Brigade: 2/Leinsters, 9/Sussex, 7/Northamptons,
                13/Middlesex and 12/Sherwood Foresters.

The key difference was that the 24th Division was a New Army Division raised from all those volunteers even as far back as the summer of 1914 although many men had joined the colours and trained during 1915 - but few if any had seen action. The 29th Division had one service battalion out of its complement of twelve while the 24th Division had nine out of its thirteen - but both would be hurled into the inferno of the Somme. The offensive potential of each division therefore varied enormously depending on the mix of regular new army units. The average division comprised eighteen thousand men divided as we have seen into three infantry brigades each of four or five battalions. The divisions were themselves then formed up into Corps commanded by a Major General and the Corps into Armies. For the hammer blow that Haig expected to deliver a decisive victory on July 1st 1916, Haig had amassed forty-five Divisions in three armies for what would be only the First Battle of The Somme.

When Jack arrived in France it was vastly different from Gallipoli. The early Spring sunshine was breaking through and the green flat fields of Flanders stretched out all around him. It was only as he started to approach the rear then front lines that the ground turned brown and white as the chalk and mud churned into the trenches that stretched across the horizon. We can gauge something of the routine and atmosphere of being in the front lines from another diary, this time that of Captain F.C. Hitcock, who was serving in the 2nd Leinsters of the 73rd Brigade:

"1st August: Bathing parades were the orders for the day. The weather was extremely hot and we kept our platoons on the banks of The Somme after we had dressed.

Mount Oriel in New South Wales, home to the Crawford-Greene family until 1911.

Edward (The Skipper) Kelly and Jack newly commissioned as Lieutenants, Summer 1914 in King Edward's Light Horse.

Jack Sherwood Kelly aged 19 as a member of The Cape Mounted Police in 1899 - top left, back row.

Jack pictured in early 1916 returned from Gallipoli having commanded the 1st. Bn. The KOSBs promoted to A/Lt.Col. on 28th October 1915 - the signs of war already beginning to show aged 35.

St. Peter's Church and No.21 Cranley Gardens, Kensington, London in 2008.

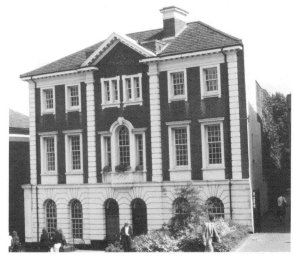

The Drill Hall, Norwich Cattle Market - regularly used by the Norfolk Yeomanry.

"A Herculean giant" - Lt.Col. Jack Sherwood Kelly standing tall in the trenches of Gallipoli in November 1915 as C.O. of 1st Bn. The KOSBs, 87th Brigade, 29th Division.

The Marriage Certificate of Jack and Nellie dated 22nd April 1916 showing Jack's age as 42 when he was in fact 36.

An aerial reconnaissance photograph of the trench lines in the Canal du Nord area of Cambrai, October 1917.

Lt.Col. Kelly as C.O. of the 1st. Bn. The Royal Inniskilling Fusiliers complete with V.C., C.M.G. and D.S.O.: note new collar dogs for his new regiment and signed "Jack".

9th August: The weather broke ; it rained heavily and the men got pretty wet. Watched shelling on the front.

11th August: D Company had 21 casualties from shellfire digging a communication trench through Trones Wood.

18th August: Orders to report to Battalion Headquarters. Found the Bn preparing to move off for action. Each man given sand-bags and bombs in addition to his cumbersome "battle order". It was a sweltering day and then men were too heavily equipped. This attack was not only a divisional operation , there was to be a general advance along the whole corps front. On our left the 14th division and on our right the 3rd Division. The Germans fully realised it's (Guillemont Ridge) importance and had turned it into an almost impregnable fortress to bar the way of the allies in their advance up the slopes of the Somme plateau in Picardy.

The men were silent and up 'til now there had only been intermittent shelling - mostly counter battery work. Suddenly a crashing roar resounded over the whole area, the bombardment of the Hun lines started punctually to the second. We passed our gunners on the way up ; they were all stripped to the waist, their sweat begrimed bodies showed one the almost superhuman effort of endurance they were making under the blazing heat. The barrage lifted at Zero hour... Simultaneously out got a line of forms from the British lines, the first wave, and disappeared into the smoke. The rattle of machine gun fire could now be heard above the roar of the guns. Laville and Handcock were killed, our gallant CO Lt col. R.A.H.Orpen-Palmer DSO was wounded along with 100 rank and file. Over 100 casualties just going up the ridge and without ever seeing the enemy.

*Streams of wounded walking and on stretchers were now beginning
to drift by ; men with smashed arms, limping and worst of all to see
- facial wounds. Among the stretcher cases were the CO and CSM
Bennett. The former was hit badly in the groin and the latter severely
in the head. I talked to them as they lay on their stretchers in a small
hollow." (Both men died soon after).* (5)

It was into just such a storm of fire that Jack Kelly led his battalion
in late June 1916. He may have been thirty-six and a strong towering
figure of inspiration but, as later photographs testify, his body was
absorbing a lot of punishment. By the end of his military career he
would have been wounded five times and gassed twice but on this
occasion he was to be badly wounded. We do not know exactly what
happened but we do know that the 29th Division at that time was
fighting in the infamous Beaumont Hamel sector of the line. If we
return to the KOSB diary we discover the phase that "…he (Kelly)
was soon severely wounded". Far more unbelievable is that in late
November 1923, whilst Jack was attempting to enter parliament
(more of which later), he was speaking at an election rally at
Shirebrook in Derbyshire only to see a woman go up to Nellie and
tell her that she was Mrs Johnson, the mother of the stretcher bearer
who saved Jack's life on the Somme when Jack was wounded by a
machine gun bullet through his left lung. The following week Jack
gave an interview with The Derbyshire Times:

*"Since 1916 I have been trying to find Johnson. I advertised
regularly for several years, made enquiries at The War Office, and
also got in touch with The Cornish Miners Association of which I
understood Johnson was a member. Last week I went to Shirebrook
and while I was speaking a woman went up to my wife and said "We
feel that your husband belongs to us." My wife answered "I don't*

quite understand - who are you?" The woman replied "My son is Jack Johnson." Johnson was not in the village at the time but an appointment was made for Col Kelly to go to his mother's house last Friday. In was in that way that he again met Jack Johnson.

"There was a good deal of handshaking and I am afraid a few tears" said Col Kelly. "You can understand my feelings when I tell you that Johnson undoubtedly saved my life. He would not leave me for a moment for 48 hours and tended me as a mother would have done. I feel my campaign in this election has been worthwhile if only for enabling me to show my gratitude to the man to who I owe so much." (6)

The sector in which Kelly's battalion was formed up was tough - every day the landscape changed as the ground was churned up and the dead bodies from weeks before were revealed and reburied in even smaller pieces. Thousands of men who died never even saw a German but ran out when the whistles sounded into the rusty barbed wire, the smell of stale water and the death-dealing chatter of machine guns. On the first day of the Somme, a month after Kelly had received his wound, a fellow unit of the KOSBs and Inniskillings had gone over the top. The 2/South Wales Borderers had been training for weeks and advanced at 08.45 am. Eight hundred officers and men, typical of many battalions doing the same thing all along the front, were simply cut to pieces. Fourteen officers and two hundred and nineteen other ranks were killed within ten minutes with another twelve officers and three hundred and seventy-four other ranks wounded within the hour. Ninety-one men were missing - blown to pieces in fractions of a second with no time to say goodbye. The terror, pain and grief was the same everywhere that day and for many days after as Haig pressed more divisions into the attack hoping to overwhelm the German lines with the bodies of devoted but ill fated men but who had long ago forgotten what they were doing there.

In June leading the attack out of the trenches, as he had done many times in Gallipoli, was the Lt. Col. of the 1/Inniskillings charging across No Man's Land. Through the smoke of the barrage that would have preceded the assault, came the voices of men advancing to their death - some encouraging those around them to keep going, others cursing the Germans to their front and somewhere in between heard above all others was the voice of Jack Kelly - his broad Irish shouts willing them on towards the Germans. Shortly afterwards Jack Kelly fell, shot through the lung - a death wound had Johnson not been there and able to carry his colonel to the rear.

Had Jack gone over on July 1st he would have died - the numbers of casualties would have overwhelmed the ability of brave men like Johnson to cope. As it was he had a chance - a slim chance of survival. All wounds were potentially fatal through disease and lack of sterile conditions. The medical staff did what they could against impossible odds but the volume of casualties was to mirror the poppies that fall from the roof of The Royal Albert Hall each year on Remembrance Day. It was impossible to comprehend so many men dying while waiting to be tended. Men were taken down the communication trenches to the rear, often still under fire, and brought to a Casualty Clearing Station - sometimes close to the front lines but often a bumpy ride a mile or so back. Arriving was one thing, getting treated was another - for late arrivals the odds were against you as the lines of walking wounded sat around behind the rows of more serious stretcher cases. No medical teams had been trained for what they encountered here and at Paschendale, Arras and many other places. The numbers were just too great to cope with.

Succumbing to shock, heart attack or simply bleeding to death was common; there were no blood transfusions and only a few operating areas.

"Strange things happened at casualty clearing stations. In some operating theatres at the heat of the push, two surgeons would be working at four to six operating tables, moving from one to the other, leaving often unqualified assistants to handle routine tasks of stitching up, dressing and even anaesthetising while they concentrated on the more delicate work of repairing damaged organs and searching for shrapnel, bullets and shell splinters buried deep in muddy wounds."

'The Roses of No Mans Land'. (7)

"I tried every means possible to restore the patient (a Colonel of tremendous size), jerking his arms round, pressing his chest and finally just when I thought I would have to give up, he took one gasp and began to breathe. When Wesley had finished with the other chap he came over to my patient and started to take his arm off at the shoulder, but as soon as the operation began he started to sink and died on the table." (8)

Jack arrived with a label with a broad red stripe indicating 'look out for danger' tied to his uniform and was taken through the crush of dead and dying men to the operating area. A few hours later and he was still alive. With Johnson sitting beside him not sleeping and tending to him for forty-eight hours, Jack was at death's doorway at every moment. Having lost a lot of blood from a lung already damaged by gas in Gallipoli Jack was very weak and dangerously ill. He was removed by train to Rouen where, remarkably, Nellie was there to meet him and tend to his wounds. We know that Nellie and her not uninfluential mother were already working for the Red Cross in London and it maybe that she received a telegram informing her of Jack's wounds. In any event either Nellie was very senior in The Red Cross and was already working in France or she was able to pull some serious strings to get herself over to Rouen - maybe it was both. The last thing the Army High Command could cope with would be thousands of loved ones and wives making their way across the Channel to tend to their loved ones so it was extremely rare for this to happen. Jack must have seemed a sorry sight to her, a husband of only two months and now severely wounded. Indeed Jack was never to recover fully from the damage done to his body in Gallipoli and The Somme.

In June 1916, Jack was moved to London to one of the 'brass hats' wards. These were for senior officers only and where the best medical treatment and sanitary conditions could be found. There were sound reasons for separating officers from men and as Lynn MacDonald explained it was easier for the other ranks not to be found alongside their officers. While in London Jack was visited by numerous friends and colleagues some of whom had attended the wedding only two months earlier. Over the summer Jack began to rebuild his strength however:

"On one occasion when he was home on leave recovering from his chest wound a friend said to him "I suppose you won't be going back out again"? To which Sherwood Kelly replied "Of course I shall, I couldn't go back to South Africa without the V.C." (9)

Though brave it was predictable and indicates that his thoughts were focussed on returning home if not permanently at least to show what he had achieved. The angry young man was still in there and even now dead set on proving everyone wrong and still getting his V.C.

During the preparations for the Somme offensive the Germans were far from silent. Instead there was a gradual increase in the hostility of the sector which, as we have seen, was widely considered to be a quiet one. As if fate were trying to bring the two men closer together again Winston Churchill now also found himself in the same area as Kelly and the 87th Brigade.

The events that brought Churchill to the front are well known. Many heads rolled in London in the wake of the Gallipoli disaster. Some were heads that deserved their fate while others were not. The debate about whether Churchill was a deserving case goes on to this day. In any event after the Dardanelles' Committee of investigation had completed its judgments in February 1916, Churchill was free to return to War Council business along with his equally distinguished colleagues. He was however shunned and his services spurned by Asquith. With his previous military background and character it should not be a surprise to learn that his main aim now became getting out to the front lines in France himself. The consternation that this action caused represents a marvellous vision of conflicting emotions amongst his political colleagues, some longing for him to disappear under some German shell while others were extremely wary of letting him loose in the British lines for fear of what might happen. In some ways the fears of this latter group were well founded as Corporal W. Morgan of 10/11th Highland Light Infantry recalled from his time in the lines near Armentieres:

"We were badly cut up at the battle of Loos in September and the 9th Scottish Division had been sent down the line to be reinforced. The casualties had been so heavy that remnants of the different regiments like the Highland Infantry and the Gordons were amalgamated. Then we went to the quietest part of the line at Armetieres, between Le

Bizet and Ploegsteert. There was hardly a shot being fired from either side, it was a case of live and let live and we were to remain here and build up strength because recruiting was very slow.

I was on my way back to Company Headquarters because I was a runner and I had just been delivering a message. When I went into the front line from the communication trench I had to turn right, but in the first bay on the left there was an officer pumping rifle grenades over at the Jerry front line. When I got back to my own stretch of trench everyone was up in arms about it and the Sergeant Major asked me if I saw who was doing it. I told him it was an officer in the next line so he went along to tell him off. When he came back he said "You'll never believe who that was. It was Churchill." After that the Jerries really let us have it and there were a lot of unnecessary casualties." (10)

The comparisons with the front line behaviours exhibited by Kelly on the cliff tops of Gallipoli are striking. Initiative, headstrong belief in the way to fight and win, disregard for the situation surrounding them and of course what might be called a reckless disregard for their own safety are just some of the parallels that can be drawn. In so many ways, therefore, the instincts and experiences of both Jack Kelly and Winston Churchill were captured by the events of wars in which they were a part. In less than three years both men would come into conflict with each other representing a titanic conflict of will and stubbornness, in which each man was to rely on similar instincts to win the struggle. Before that however, Jack Kelly very nearly did not survive the wounds he received in June 1916.

(1)   The East London Daily Despatch, 22nd April, 1916

(2)   'The Ladies Field', February 9th, 1918. p.369

(3)   KOSB's diary p.179

(4)   Gliddon. G., 'When The Barrage Lifts'

(5)   Hitchcock Capt. F.C. "Stand To - A Diary of the trenches 1915-1918. (Gliddon Books, 1988). p.109

(6)   The Derbyshire Times, 3rd December 1923

(7)   MacDonald Lyn. 'The Roses of No Mans Land' (MacMillan)

(8)   Ibid p.177 from the memoirs of Capt. The Rev. L. Pearson, Chaplain to Number 44 CCS

(9)   'The Times', 19th August, 1931

(10)   MacDonald Lyn, Ibid p.124

CHAPTER SIX

*'One mark of a great man is the power of making lasting
impressions upon the people he meets'*
- Winston S. Churchill, (1874-1965)

THE MAN REVEALS HIMSELF, 1916-1917: CAMBRAI AND THE VICTORIA CROSS

The traumatic events of 1916 must have affected Nellie very deeply but they also showed her the true nature of the man she had married. Difficult to love, Jack was equally difficult to hold down and the events on the Somme proved to Nellie that the devil may care attitude so attractive in Jack was also his potential nemesis at any time.

Over what was a very hot summer in London, Nellie sat beside Jack every day until he was well enough to return to Cranley Gardens. Her tall, strong and dashing husband of almost four months had been reduced to a weak and thin shadow of himself but at least she had him to herself - for the longest period that they were ever to experience. The options open to Jack now were either to be invalided out of the army, he had after all survived more wounds than the average, or to get himself fit to return to the front lines. Over these weeks it must have been the subject of many a conversation between them over what the future could hold. From Nellie's perspective, Jack could now apply for a job in The City, perhaps build a home together, if they moved quickly enough maybe even start a family. From Jack's perspective it is unlikely that any of these thoughts even entered his head. The settling down, raising a family and rat race of life that Jack saw around him was just not going to be for him. The wind in his hair, the excitement of challenge and the need to vent his passions could only be served by a return to active duty. Before that however the two of them did discuss a convalescent trip back to South Africa - which was attractive to Jack. Here at last was a way of demonstrating that at the age of thirty six he had, if not made his fortune, made his mark and reputation. Perhaps it was to show his father that he was worthwhile and misunderstood, perhaps it was to show the whole of South Africa what they had in Jack. In any event, in July 1916 Nellie and Jack Kelly embarked for South Africa - partly to recover Jack's health but also to recruit for the army whose need for men, after the bloodbath of the Somme, was as acute as ever.

The accepted price for glory is death. This has been understood by military men embarked on gladiatorial combat ever since men first bore arms. However the rewards can be many and varied. Jack's instinctive character as we have seen from his very early days was to play to the gallery, partly to demand attention but also to put himself and his body on the line. If fighting in Somaliland, The Boer Wars and now The Great War was for a cause, then the trip to South Africa was to reap the rewards of a gallery eager to bestow laurels upon heroes. So it was that Jack arrived to a blizzard of newspaper interviews, tours, speeches and trips, lunches, dinners and salutations. Advanced warning of the hero's return had been telegraphed to Cape Town where Jack and Nellie landed in the last week of July 1916. Jack's ego probably overtook his interest in Nellie somewhere on the two week cruise and was let loose on arrival. Our evidence for this assessment is based sadly on their divorce proceedings in April 1919. Here we are given a valuable snapshot of the type of relationship that Nellie, the kind, gentle and intelligent woman admired by all her friends, and Jack endured.

Interestingly the court hearing, surely not surprisingly, stated that:

"In July (1916) they both went out to South Africa. Difficulties arose there. He said he was tired of his marriage as he was giving up his liberty. They returned to England ." (1)

What are we to make of this? All relationships encounter problems, highs and lows, incompatible elements and compromises but it seems incredible that after only four months - most of which Jack had not even been with Nellie, he felt constrained. They had not even had a marriage and now Jack wanted it to end. This must have been devastating for Nellie especially as it was not actually true that they were incompatible at all but that Jack was just selfish in the extreme - the product of an over bearing and over confident personality driven to be something great. But it was also clear that he enjoyed the adoration now thrown at him from a myriad of female admirers as another section of the divorce proceedings indicated:

"Some of the women her husband had previously rather admired began to exercise the old fascination over him." (2)

Jack had left South Africa only three years previously a complete unknown. He returned a dashing, uniformed and medalled Lt. Colonel in the British Army - a hero, a generous benefactor of hospitals and most importantly of all - unavailable to women as he was also now married. This explosive combination was not lost on Jack who perhaps saw Nellie as rather an unnecessary obstacle to his ability to be available, circulate and no doubt exploit. Nellie must have felt completely alone. She had married a man whom she idolised. London was awash with handsome men in uniform but Nellie had been swept off her feet by the strong, cavalier and confident Jack, with his Colonel's uniform to boot. She had elevated him in her family and in London society. She had rescued him and nursed him when he was near death and now she had followed him to South Africa only to be pushed away and abandoned as he basked in the superficial glory of a moth to the brightest of lights - and like a moth he would eventually burn. Perhaps Nellie could see this. Like many women of understanding and sensitivity, she recognized the naivety and vanity of a brave but fragile man. He did not know what he was doing to a woman of a substance beyond his understanding and it would be an injustice to Nellie for us to allow her devotion to remain silent in this history.

By the beginning of September 1916 it was time for Jack and Nellie to make the long and no doubt painful trip back to England. By mid September Nellie had arrived home to Cranley Gardens and the support of her friends, family and mother. Jack on the other hand immediately reported for duty and waited to be posted back to active duty commanding the 1st Battalion of The Inniskillings who were still serving on the front lines on France. Jack was showing to Nellie that he was untamable and unstoppable - at least at this stage of his life. Before Jack could get back to the front however on 29th November 1916 he had to make the first of a number of visits to Buckingham Palace to meet the King for the award of his DSO. We can wonder at what such an occasion did to further heighten Jack's sense of self importance and success - as if such elevation was necessary. Even after the award of the DSO and a new ribbon to add to the impressive array already on this still young man's chest, there was still no call to the front. This would have been partly due to a relapse in Jack's health in the December of 1916. Still in London at Christmas, Jack and Nellie had agreed to work at their relationship. They were to be seen on the London social circuit - Nellie was even making a name for herself as a leading figure in the Red Cross, helping with the dispatch of tens of thousands of Christmas parcels to the troops in France that year - what are now very collectable small brass tins. By the end of November 1916 Jack had been posted to Duddingston Camp near Edinburgh, back to the home of the KOSBs, but all was not good. In the first place he had reverted to his substantive rank of Major as he no longer commanded a battalion but even worse when he arrived to report to the 3rd Battalion he discovered that the 1st battalion was also in the process of arriving in the same camp. Clearly he was not wanted back in the 1st battalion otherwise he would have been able to meet up with them but equally this should have been a good opportunity to catch up on old acquaintances. Not so. In a letter hidden amongst his many papers in The National Archives in Kew we find the following:

'To : Commanding Officer 3rd King's Own Scottish Borderers

5.XII.16

Sir,

I have the honour to request that you will recommend this my application for a transfer to The 10th Norfolk Reserve Battalion. My chief reason for making this request is that for 7th months I commanded the 1st KOSB in Gallipoli and France with the rank of Lieut. Colonel and find that some officers and many of the men at present in camp who served with the 1st battalion during my command.

I am Sir your obedient servant,

J. Sherwood Kelly
Major.'

On one level it is understandable that having held the rank of Lt. Colonel and now to be returned to Major could seem a small embarrassment which Jack wanted to avoid. However on another level it may well have been that he was so unpopular with the remaining officers of the 1st battalion that his presence in the mess, where he may well now be junior to many, made his presence in the camp acutely difficult. Either way a sign of his desperation was not to simply ask for a transfer but to ask to be sent to the 10th battalion of the Norfolk's - almost an impossible request to deny and all in all this short letter offers us a valuable insight into the inner fragility of the so called colossus.

Despite the war, the tragic losses on The Somme that year and the food and fuel shortages, London was alive and making the best of Christmas 1916. For Jack there were still parties to attend raising money for hospitals and returning heroes and the restaurants still managed to bring game and supplies into town from the countryside. The hotels were busy and life in many respects went on as normal. The London Gentlemen's Clubs too were active and, as though to validate his new found place in the social order, Jack was made a member of The Authors' Club. An odd choice given that this particular club liked its members to be published authors however it was probably achieved through contacts of either Nellie or her brother William. Later references to Jack's life in the 1920s state that he was a resident member of the club - making it his home for want of other accommodation. We can safely assume that Jack and Nellie were on good terms over those winter months and that Jack was resident in Cranley Gardens. Whatever Christmas gifts he received that year however were topped off by the award of yet another medal - just what Nellie did not need to calm the bravado of her husband.

The Distinguished Order of St. Michael and St. George came into existence in 1818 as a response to Britain acquiring the protectorate over The Ionian Islands in The Aegean Sea. Initially this award was restricted to "subjects which His Majesty may hold high in confidential stations in the Mediterranean world". However, as the British Empire expanded at such a rate of knots during the 19th century, the Order had grown to be used to recognize the service of those resident or even native of the lands which they served. By 1900 the Order was being given to many who had given valuable service in either foreign or colonial affairs. In addition to the medal itself came the full paraphernalia of officers of the order and even a Chapel in St Paul's Cathedral - so vital was the support on the ground needed to subdue and control the creaking empire. There were three classes of award:

First Class or Knight Grand Cross (GCMG)

Second Class or Knight Commander (KCMG)

Third Class or Companion (CMG)

For each of the levels there was a stated limitation on the number of holders. For the CMG this was set at 600 and on January 1st 1917 A/Lt Col Jack Sherwood Kelly, Norfolk Regiment (for he was still on attachment) was awarded the CMG for services to the Empire - most likely his recruiting drive in South Africa the previous summer.

The Somme offensives had failed in their key objectives and the slaughter had been both inexcusable and appalling. During 1916 some four hundred thousand British casualties had either been buried, patched up and returned to the front or were recovering in hospitals all over Britain. Shell shock was still a new phenomenon and until it was understood and accepted, court martials and executions were running at dozens a month. If the flower of the British Army had been lost in the summer of 1914 then the rest of the petals and stem had been destroyed in 1916 - what was left was an army unrecognizable from that which had entered the conflict two years previously.

In February 1917 the newly decorated Lt. Col. Kelly received his orders to rejoin the Royal Inniskilling Fusiliers and the diary of the regiment records that on 29th March 1917 Major J.S.Kelly once more took over command of the 1st Battalion from Lt. Col. R.R.Willis VC. So Kelly was back, well decorated, maybe a little wiser and where he wanted to be as part of the British front lines in France. The transition from a life in London to the mud, blood and hardship of France must have been dramatic but this is where his heart still was. London life and rest for the last nine months had not softened him in any way - he was what he was and he was at home with this unit far more than he was with the KOSBs in Gallipoli or indeed with Nellie. "Fighting like Kilkenny cats" as they were in the fields of mud, the men of the Inniskillings lived up to their regimental motto of *Nec Aspera Terrant - By difficulties Undaunted.*

April saw the next major British offensives of 1917 with large scale attacks at Vimy and Arras - on the Oise/Rheims sectors respectively. These in their own ways were major battles of The Great War although they are overshadowed by their Somme predecessor. They were however extensions of the same strategic plan and were beaten off in the same way with huge losses. The French too were far from inactive. Having held Verdun at terrible cost, they also pushed forward with their 'Nivelle Offensive' and yet another forty thousand lives were lost in the ensuing slaughter. It was beginning to seem that the Generals had no idea how to break the deadlock except to wear out each side until there were no men left. The French 16th Army experienced a series of mutinies which were ruthlessly suppressed with many executions. Then the scene changed forever. The German strategy of unrestricted submarine warfare, borne out of desperation to try to starve Britain out of a war which they were stubbornly refusing to lose in France, served only one purpose and that was eventually to bring America into the war. President Wilson had done all he could to maintain America's isolationist stance but such a war at sea was a war on all mankind and the sleeping giant was awakened. Now it was only a matter of time before the men and materiel of America would start to arrive in France. It was badly needed as on the Eastern Front the internal decay and ultimate collapse of Tsarist Russia had commenced and troops began to throw down their arms. The communists saw the chance of revolution in this archaic and anarchic country.

In the meantime the British were expected to continue to apply pressure to the Germans. The French were consolidating under their new hero Marshall Petain (the 'hero' of Verdun) and so Haig once more devised another major offensive to try to force a hole in the German front through which his forces could flow. In June 1917 it was Ypres and Passchendaele - two names that live in infamy alongside the most murderous of all battles. Two hundred and fifty thousand British troops struggled through the rain, mud, blood and stench of the fields around them to gain but a few miles and again they failed to break though.

For the line officers the situation was clear. There was no solution though brute force and a seemingly overwhelmingly strong barrage of artillery followed by close infantry support was certainly not the answer. The cemeteries of Flanders held well over a million men who bore testimony to that. How far and yet how little distance we had come since those first opening shots fired by The Norfolks when they first met the German troops advancing through Belgium in the 24th August 1914. It must have seemed very tempting for Jack to speak out at this senseless waste of life and good men. After all he had a reputation for this since to his youth together with an unorthodox style - where had both of these traits gone? Perhaps it was exactly that his obligation to lead his men from his new position as a senior officer showed him that difficult decisions were indeed the privilege and obligation of rank. Equally, the British establishment of which he was now a part expected loyalty in return for the rewards of rank and status that it had given him. For the time being he gave it.

Another smaller scale assault had been planned for the Cambrai sector. The date of the attack had been set for November 20th 1917 and central to this was the introduction of a new weapon designed to win the war - the Mark One tank. The allied troops in this sector were faced by German positions that had been dug and created over years, an almost impregnable wall of defences as part of the so called Hindenburg Line after the senior commander in that sector (the future Field Marshall Hindenburg who was to become Chancellor of Germany and eventually hand over power to Adolf Hitler - himself a Corporal in Cambrai at that time).

Some two years previously Colonel Fuller had suggested a plan to use the tank in a raid. It had failed due to the fact that the tanks had been dispersed. This time they were to be used in a group - a forerunner of the tactics employed by the Germans in the Second

World War. General Julian Byng of 4th Army proposed the plan to Haig. The attack on Cambrai was to be a small raid with the objective being:

"...to destroy the enemy's personnel and guns, to demoralize and disorganize him and not to capture ground."

The whole assault was to take eight to twelve hours in total with nine battalions of tanks and three divisions of infantry. Initially Haig was not impressed with the idea as his focus was on Passcendaele but eventually Byng was given approval for his 'raid'. It is important that we fully grasp the intention at Cambrai because perversely it was the limitations on this assault which prevented the one attack which had broken through from being the breakthrough the High Command had been looking for. Perhaps given the perversity of the struggle to date we should not be surprised.

Given the clear limitations of aim there was no need for the staff officers behind the lines to prepare for a major development of the attack with reserves and further waves of troops. The plan was to attack on a very concentrated front of only five miles between the Canal du Nord and St Quentin Canal. The town of Cambrai would then be encircled and Bourlon Ridge captured. The entire tank corps (soon to be renamed the Royal Tank Regiment) was to be deployed with two hundred and sixteen tanks in the initial advance with a further ninety-six in reserve. The whole was to be supported by fourteen squadrons from The Royal Flying Corps (the later Royal Air Force). Although not an enthusiast for the plan, Haig could see that new tactics were going to be deployed here by Byng which meant the co-coordinated use of aircraft (to cover the noise of the advance of the tanks) together with infantry and tanks advancing together - in this sense the Cambrai plan was new for the time and a forerunner of World War Two with mixed arm interaction and Byng was optimistic of success. This was more than could be said of some of his senior officers. For example General Harper commanding the 51st Highland Division did not even trust the machine gun, having tried to hold up its introduction into the British Army, let alone the tank. Harper's view was that the plan was "a fantastic and most unmilitary scheme." (4)

Nevertheless the plan was to go ahead and General Byng briefed his Divisional Major Generals who in turn briefed their Brigadiers who in turn briefed the Colonels commanding their battalions who in turn briefed the Majors and Captains commanding their companies who in turn briefed their platoon and section commanders who in turn explained to the men in the mud how they were once more going to advance into German machine guns and win the war without being killed. For Lt. Col. Kelly this had meant being ordered to move his battalion on the 17th November from Basseux up to their FUP (Forming Up Point) by the 19th as the regimental diary recorded:

"Marching through Gouzecourt early in the morning, the Inniskillings had a dramatic hint of the nature of the surprise being prepared for the enemy. The village was quiet but the houses contained no sleeping soldiers, instead they sheltered tanks." (5)

The task of 29th Division was to act in support of the 12th, 20th and 6th Divisions who had 'brown' and 'blue' lines to reach in the first two days. If they made these objectives then the 29th was to move through their lines and press on to Reach the 'red' lines which were the final objectives and then hold them until reinforced. For Kelly's battalion this meant moving up in close support of the 2/South Wales

Borderers whose objectives were the Marcoing Copse and the vital crossing points over the Canal du Nord - if these could be taken then the advance into the German rear and Cambrai itself was possible and utter confusion could be inflicted on the German lines.

In their usual fashion the German commanders were well informed before the attack began. Their spy network was far better than in World War Two and they knew the date of the attack, the direction and the units involved. The attack was preceded by the usual noise and bustle of men coming into the front lines and the increased activity. The actual attack began on the very cold and very damp morning of 20th November 1917. The men were awakened and moved into lines - both front and coming up the rear communication and support trenches around 3am ready for the 06.00 start. Tired, cold and scared they stirred, scratched their eyes trying to awaken their minds to the fact that they could be dead and dying within three hours and started looking at each other - some with the dead eyes of those beyond caring and some wide eyed and frightened at the prospect of losing a life that they had not yet even lived. Their hated muddy holes now seemed like five star hotels into which they wished they could return and hide but there was nowhere to go but up the line. Sergeants and Sergeant Majors did what they were paid to do - a bit of humour a bit of nagging and bit of fatherly advice and a bit of barking under quieted breath - his familiar voice more often than not being the key to discipline and the containment of fear. The cold wet sludge on their feet as they walked over wooden boards trodden on by thousands of men before them who would not return like a rite of passage into hell. Men wet themselves, soiled themselves, puked and waited.

Then it erupted. Like a hundred times before men like Jack Kelly blew warm air into frozen hands and whistles and jumped out of their skin as at 06.00 hours one thousand and three guns opened fire. The noise, like the thundercrack of a volcano finally blowing its top, saw thousands of shells fall onto German lines all around Cambrai and the two canals and told the Germans that within minutes the infantry would be on their way towards them. The German troops knew how to cope. Although many died being blown into irredeemable pieces by direct hits, far more ran deep underground where only collapsing walls and dugouts could threaten them and bury them in black, cold and forgotten tombs. The artillery in fact helped shelter the Germans far more than kill them as the shells tore up the ground, mixed it with mud, filled the area with huge shell holes that the advancing men and tanks would now have to cross. As the smoke and noise of the shelling did its work so too did the cold thick mists coming off the water from the canals and a scene from a cold Dante's inferno began to be painted onto the landscape in front of Jack's battalion.

As he had done in Gallipoli, the giant Colonel with his scarf around his neck to protect his chest, maybe a gift from Nellie, walked up and down the line encouraging the men and looking at the attitude of his young officers - slapping a back here and there and passing a joke or two. He must have been an inspiration - this was what he did best and for certain Jack gave off that innate confidence and certainty only found in a natural leader that this was not only going to be a successful attack but also they would all survive. Final checks to weapons, fixing of bayonets - almost the last order the men would hear - and then coming up behind them the squeak and creak of steel tracks of the tanks struggling through the mud.

The noise and roar of the tanks was new and their engines puffed out acrid smoke to add to the carnage of battle and then the whistles blew and the men shouted and charged up and out of their trenches all along the line. As one battalion left another came up, filled the places where others had been standing and they too then took their turn running through the bodies of those smashed in front of them. Initially the attack went well, very well. The Royal Flying Corps did their stuff overhead and the tanks rolled through and past the front ranks and on and into the German lines. The German troops had no choice but to either be crushed by the tanks or run. As Captain D.G.Browne reflected in 1920:

"The immediate onset of the tanks was inevitably overwhelming. The German outposts, dazed or annihilated by the sudden deluge of shells were overrun in an instant. The triple belts of barbed wire were crossed as if they had been belts of nettles and 350 pathways were sheared in them for the infantry. The defenders of the line running panic stricken, casting away arms and equipment...over the whole southern half of the battlefield the defence had collapsed and this area was virtually cleared by midday." (6)

The initial assaults therefore went incredibly well, far better than anyone expected. The only place that the attack faltered was in front of the 51st Highland Division where by all accounts the sceptical General Harper had instructed his infantry to hold back from close support with the tanks with the effect that once the tanks had passed the German lines some German infantry simply set up their machine guns again and took on the advancing infantry as normal while the tanks continued on alone and were cut off and destroyed. Thus the 51st Division stalled at its first objective - the village of Flesquires - and forty tanks were lost in this sector. However elsewhere the advance and shock of the tanks was going well and by mid morning many of the first and second line objectives had been reached. By the evening an advance of 8 km had been secured - more in one day than in the entire three month battle of Passchendaele (Third Battle of Ypres).

At H+1 The Inniskillings were ordered up into the line to the village of Villiers Plouich. On the way close artillery fire started to fall on them and their first casualties were absorbed. With the news that the blue lines had also been taken the entire 29th division was activated and ordered forward to advance through the troops in front of them. All three brigades advanced on their map bearings in arrowhead formations walking through mangled rusty barbed wire with body parts draped from them, through mud mixed with blood and water on into the German lines where many dead and dying men could be seen and then past many of the tanks - around one hundred and eighty tanks were lost on that first day across the five mile front of which sixty-five had been destroyed by German guns and over seventy had broken down but they had done their job well. As if by a stroke of fate it was the 87th Brigade that was ordered to take the divisional point and within that Lt. Colonel Jack Sherwood Kelly DSO, CMG and his battalion was ordered to lead the way for the whole division. Why were they chosen? There may never be an answer but it is a fair guess that if you were the Brigade Commander and you wanted a fire breathing and fearless devil to lead the Brigade forward as far as possible through the mud and devastation then who better than Jack Sherwood Kelly and the 1st Battalion of the Royal Inniskilling Fusiliers?

By 10.30 am they had come up behind the South Wales Borderers who had lost a significant number of men to get to this point. Moving through Kelly ordered his line companies to move fast towards the enemy rear lines and dugouts. By 11.30 they were within sight of the Canal and through the smoke, mud, mist and gunfire it was possible to see the crossing places and icy cold water which were the objective some fifty yards away. The little stone bridge over the misty canal was vital and as the regimental history records:

"When the canal crossings had been secured, the Inniskillings were to cross the canal and, with the help of the tanks, seize their allotted position of the red line and consolidate. This portion east of the main road to Cambrai was just beyond the ridge of Masnieres and was part of the Rumilly system of trenches of the Hindenburg Line." (7)

The Germans had run back to the other side of the Canal bank and had already set up their machine guns in some ruined farmhouses and in the banks overlooking the Canal. It was immediately clear to Jack that to press on meant pushing his men into a withering machine gun and artillery fire but to stop meant that not only would the Battalion advance stop but also that of the Brigade and behind that the whole division - he had to get across that canal somehow and it would almost certainly mean death for any officer leading such a charge - so he did just that.

Keeping the momentum of the advance going was vital. The South Wales Borderers had been advancing all morning but had stopped as German rifle and machine gun fire hit the bridge. The men behind him were good but they were still men. It was now 12.00 midday and if they stopped they would start to think about where they were and what was in front of him so within seconds Kelly ordered his machine guns forward to start laying down covering fire on the bank opposite, then called up his leading company shouting so that everyone could hear him that under smoke they were going to rush the bank charge over the crossing places and remove the Germans from the other side - and they were going to do it now - and he was going to lead them.

The morning mists had now cleared and by the time Kelly ordered the charge at 12.25 a little autumn sun was poking through the grey clouds and smoke of the battlefield and glinting on the water. There was still some grass here and there on the bank and Kelly could see the helmets of the grey clad German soldiers running from place to place fully aware of what was about to happen. And then it did. The Inniskillings machine gunners started laying down heavy fire onto the German positions only a few metres away over the canal. Kelly and about seventy men from A company edged forward as close as they could to the start of the gently rising slope that led onto the bridge and then it was "UP AND AT THEM". Leading the charge Kelly felt the whistle of bullets passing by him, some thumping into the mud and others into men who groaned or simply fell to ground like sacks as bullets tore into their bodies. The hobnails in the British boots coupled with the screams and shouts of a bayonet charge, perhaps with eyes closed, smashed over the bridge and into a German trench. Bayonets were driven into chests and stomachs of the defenders and Kelly hit the ground - they were over - but only just. Calling for more men to cross Kelly was then up again calling on the men around him to follow him a few more yards in and around the buildings to clear them. By 1.00 Kelly was sending runners back to Brigade Headquarters to inform them that the bridge was secure, Kelly now looked to his front to see that the ground ran upwards to a small ridge running across their front. The Germans were now on that ridge hastily digging in and beginning to fire down onto both the bank behind him and onto his new positions on the German side of the bridge. Unless he cleared the ridge he would not be able to hold the bridge.

By now most of the battalion was over the bridge and fanning out to his left and right. To the left British troops of another unit were starting to fall back to the canal so it was clear to Kelly that the battalion needed to advance up the slope and push the Germans off the ridge. He gave orders for the battalion advance up the slope. What was left of A and B Companies who had initially rushed the ridge would take the front with C and D companies in support and ready to move through if A and B faltered. Whether Jack was feeling the effects of his old chest wounds (both gas and bullet) is not known but even if he was he was still unstoppable. This was perhaps the tightest squeeze he had ever been in and the sense of excitement and opportunity filled him with energy. Kelly shouted the order to advance and immediately men began falling around him as they ran towards and up the ridge in front. Officers shouted, Sergeants shouted, men screamed. Yard by yard the Inniskillings made it up the slope but then he noticed how his left flank had disappeared and stopped moving. A runner scrambled over to him through the mud to say that they had fallen into a ravine full of barbed wire and were being cut to pieces. Jack told his second in command to keep the advance moving and scrambled over to his left. About twenty meters of barbed wire lay in front of his men who were at once trying to cut through it and fall back. Jack shouted for a Lewis Gun team to join him and they moved to their left and started to cut and crawl a path through the wire. They were being shot at all the time but the rest of the company were laying down heavy fire on the Germans to keep their heads down. After ten hard, grueling minutes Jack and his team of three, covered from head to toe in mud and not a few scratches from the wire, were through and able to crawl up the slope, set up their gun and start ripping into the German dugouts from the side. At the same time his company charged through the wire and made it to the top of the slope. Behind them about forty men lay on the ground in and around the wire, dead and wounded.

The battalion now had command of the ridge and was digging into what only minutes before had been German holes, mud and water. They rested for a few minutes and surveyed where they had got to. To their left and right they could see British units fighting their way forward and the carcasses of tanks were everywhere. Close by were the bodies of around a hundred German soldiers interspersed with his own men, and first aid parties were making their way around those many wounded down by the barbed wire. However to his front Jack could see a whole series of German dugouts in no particular order, some of them starting to crackle fire towards him, and behind them about two hundred yards away was the Marcoing - Rumilly Road. There was no time to stop and admire their work because to their front lay yet more pits, and Kelly ordered the supporting companies to move through and continue the attack in the same way. Quickly reorganizing and reforming A and B companies they moved up in support. This second assault was also successful; the men were well blooded and Kelly used their blind courage to the full. Ordering the men to dig in, Kelly ran across the field under fire to join them. They were nearly at the main road and far ahead of where they should have been.

Looking around him, Jack could see the faces and uniforms of half the men that had started the attack two hours before - the other half were either dead, wounded or dying. Tired, covered in sweat and mud the men lay against the muddy banks of their holes gasping for breath and wondered what their CO would do next. His options were to dig in and wait for the rest of the brigade to catch up, or withdraw back to the ridge for better protection. To his left and right Kelly would have been able to see that he had pressed on further than any other unit, and was already very exposed. To his front he could see the Church tower of Cambrai and the frantic movement here and there of German soldiers - either preparing to attack him or waiting for the Inniskillings to continue the assault. Suddenly at that moment a mass of German machine gun fire began thudding into the ground and his men. As if being determined to get himself killed on this day, Kelly grabbed the nearest junior officer and shouted at the twenty or so men near him, ordering an immediate charge straight at the pits from which the heavy fire was originating. It was a dash of only forty yards but twelve men fell into the mud with horrendous wounds. Regardless of this, Kelly continued screaming at his men to keep going, and miraculously he jumped into the pits feet first, immediately shot two Germans through the chest, punched a third and watched as the rest of the Germans threw up their hands in surrender. Due to this brave, successful endeavor he had captured five machine guns and forty-six prisoners, with a further twenty or so dead on the ground - some of whom had been bayoneted by his men. To the relief of his men he then ordered the entire battalion to retire 100 yards back from the road, and dig in for the night ahead. By five o'clock in the afternoon, his four companies had dug themselves into the muddy ground and made contact with the rest of the brigade to their left and right. What Kelly did not realize was that he was the furthermost British unit on this first day of the Cambrai attack.

During the night and in between heavy shelling, reports came in to Kelly giving details of how the battalion had fared that day. The Inniskillings had taken fifty four prisoners, a further five officers, and had killed over fifty Germans. However their own casualties had been high. One officer and twenty men had been killed, but the mauling on the wire had left five officers and a hundred and sixteen men wounded - over thirty percent of the battalion's strength. A further five men had disappeared in the shelling. However they had achieved all their objectives; crossed the canal and pushed on the best part of half a mile further than expected. During the early hours of the morning it was clear that there were problems, the advance had gone better than expected and so there were no reserves available to force through their positions, and most of the tanks used on that first day were out of action.

Back home in London and across Britain, church bells rang out and newspapers celebrated this major victory, but the reality was very different. As Liddle Hart pointed out, Third Army, within whose sector Cambrai lay, had only six divisions available for the attack and no reserve because a breakthrough was not expected. For the next five days Jack Kelly and the rest of 29th division sat exposed to increasingly heavy gunfire and lost many men who had made it through the first day of the attack. Kelly, as always, had acted on instinct - he had driven his men forward quite willingly accepting the dangers, because he could see an opportunity. Further back behind the lines the senior commanders could not. Paradoxically it was the reverse of most of WW1, where commanders had thrown men forward in hopeless attacks on impregnable positions when the men in the field could see it was pointless but they had done their duty never the less. This time it was the men that could see an opportunity and the senior commanders were not there to exploit it.

General Luddendorf fully expected his lines to be broken by the British at any moment after 29th November and issued instructions for a general retreat. The official German account states that, 'a wide gap remained open for many hours completely unoccupied between Masinires and Crevecoer'. Had allied troops and tanks moved up during the night then who knows how the course of the entire war might have changed at that point. Instead, Kelly and his men remained in the lines alone for five days and the Germans saw a miraculous opportunity to save what seemed like a desperate situation. Five German divisions moved into the area over the next twenty four hours and another six started to move there.

By 25th November, 1/Inniskillings needed a rest. 1/Essex came up to relieve them and a changeover was affected during that evening. The Inniskillings began moving to the rear lines of the 29th Divisional sector. It was increasingly apparent to many officers that in front of them the Germans were preparing a massive build up of forces. The warning signs were everywhere. General Snow commanding VII Corps was even able to announce the date and location of the attack while General Jeudwine of 55th Division supported this view and cited a list of collaborative evidence as a serious warning to his superiors such as 'very active enemy artillery zeroing in on previously ignored targets as a precursor to heavy bombardment, vastly increased enemy air reconnaissance and air attacks on rear troop concentrations'. Yet, incredibly, all this seemed to make no impression until it was too late. On November 30th, only 10 days after reeling under the first day of the allied attack on Cambrai, the Germans unleashed their own offensive. Their recovery had been born out of necessity while their success was as a result of mistakes by the British High Command. Without adequate reserves or preparation for the obvious, British troops were forced back to their original position. The fact that the Germans did not break through altogether was again in part, due to the experience courage and determination of 29th Division who 'held fast our positions intact and organized and made a defensive flank to link up with the units on their right which had fallen back'. On November 30th the attack came to its lines and nine assaults, four of them heavy ones, were repelled. The front held by the Division was now double in length, though casualties had cut its strength by half. It was desirable to shorten the line a little by withdrawing the line to west of Masnieres, a post which was now surrounded on three sides. The canal crossings were still held.' However by 3rd December Haig ordered a withdrawl back to the original start lines and all the efforts of 29th Division and losses of forty-five thousand casualties had been in vain.

So it was that the British press back home once more had to leap into acrobatic convolutions and the failure at Cambrai became eclipsed by the gallant defence with headlines such as:

"HOW THE GERMANS MASSED TWENTY DIVISIONS AGAINST THE SHARP BRITISH SALIENT AND TEMPORARILY FORCED OUR LINE"

And so a bungled attack became a celebration of stoic defence. Byng even blamed the men not the staff officers:

"I attribute the reason for the local successes on the part of the enemy to one cause and one cause alone, namely the lack of training on the part of junior officers and NCOs and men."

Presumably the fact that any experienced officer, NCO or man had already been murdered by previous pointless battles planned by men such as Byng was not seen as the root of this deficiency.

All of this was of course of no help to the men now buried in shallow graves in the cold and wet ground around the crossing points of the canal. They had given their all and followed Kelly forward in faith and courage. Kelly too had given his all. Five days in the wet and bitter November cold, the smoke, mist and coupled with the emotional strain of first the attack and then holding on to their positions had taken its toll and he collapsed. His lungs had given way to cold and pneumonia. On December 4th he was sent down the lines to Treport Hospital and the battalion was handed over to Major J.R.C. Dent. Once again Jack made it back to England arriving in London on December 17th. Also once again Nellie was there to welcome him home to Cranley Gardens and convalescence over the Christmas break. Her love for Jack superseded any doubts that either she or her family had for his commitment to her or the marriage. Visitors over December included Major J.S.Felix who had come to not only share a glass of Madeira with Jack and Nellie , whom he knew through his work with the Red Cross, but also to see the man for himself. Felix had at times been as close to Nellie as anyone. He held a candle for her and consoled her during Jack's periods at the front and also during the difficult times at home. Felix was concerned for Nellie and her brother William trusted him and secretly hoped that should separation and divorce eventually be the only answer, that Felix would be there for her.

On one particular visit Felix had also been entrusted with an envelope addressed to Jack. It contained a letter from The War Office informing Jack that he had been recommended and immediately confirmed for the award of The Victoria Cross for his actions on November 20th. Only a few months before, Jack had told Nellie that the only way he would leave the army was to win the Victoria Cross. Half said in jest and half of course meant, Jack had now done what he said he needed to do. In early January the newspapers carried reports of Jack's bravery and on 11th January 1918 the London Gazette carried the news of the award along with a further eighteen winners on the VC. The citation read:

"John Sherwood Kelly CMG, DSO. Major (Acting Lt. Col.) Norfolk Regiment commanding a battalion of The Royal Inniskillings Fusiliers. For most conspicuous bravery and fearless leading when a party of men of another unit detailed to cover the passage of the Canal by his battalion were held up on the near side of the canal by heavy rifle fire directed at the bridge. Lt. Col. Sherwood Kelly at once ordered covering fire and personally led the leading company of his battalion across the canal, and after crossing, reconnoitered under heavy rifle and machine gun fire the high ground held by the enemy. The left flank of his battalion advancing to the assault of this objective was held up by a thick belt of wire, whereupon he crossed to that flank, and with a Lewis Gun team, forced his way under heavy fire through obstacles, got the gun into position on the far side and covered the advance of his battalion through the wire, thereby enabling them to capture the position. Later he personally led a charge against some pits from which a heavy fire was being directed on his men, captured the pits together with five machine guns and 46 prisoners, and killed a large number of the enemy. The great gallantry displayed by this officer throughout the day inspired the greatest confidence in his men and it was mainly due to his example and devotion to duty that his battalion was enabled to capture and hold their objective." (8)

Whatever judgments can be made about Kelly, his fiery temper, his clashes with authority and his stubbornness one cannot argue with his courage in the face of overwhelming odds. That day in November Kelly, his body already beaten and bruised by serious wounds that had only just healed, threw himself at an enemy determined to kill him - not once but numerous times as if to taunt death. His men saw a hero, a giant of a man who pushed them on to victory and was always there at the very front ready to die for them and their cause.

Far greater in stature than the DSO, the award of the VC was a major event in anyone's life and that of the nation. Clearly the relationship between Nellie and Jack had stabilised over the last six months, consequently Nellie made all the arrangements and ensured that as many members of his family that could be found were invited to the ceremony. Nellie also organized an after ceremony reception at Cranley Gardens where members of her own family, including her mother, would be present.

Outside Buckingham Palace friends and family waited for Jack and Nellie to emerge into the cold grey air of a typical London morning on 23rd January 1918 - ten days after his 38th birthday. At 11.15 they came out and walked across the gravel in front of the palace. In the photograph that we have of the very moment that Jack joined three of his brothers with Nellie beside him we see the biggest smile from the man that we have on record. Holding the medal and box high for all to see we can only imagine what thoughts ran through his head both on a superficial but also a deeper level. These minutes and this day was the high point of his life. Right back in the Boer War as a teenager he had dreamt of a Victoria Cross and now he was holding his own. Was it really only about taking on the world and proving it wrong or was it showing his father and family that he could take it and stand tall - or maybe it was the cause - any cause as we know - that spurred him on and on? In an earlier age Jack would have been a soldier of fortune, a cavalier, a man that other men would follow or that more unscrupulous men would use for their own ends. He did not know it then, but the second of these was now waiting for him in the guise of Winston Churchill who already had plans afoot that would suck Jack Kelly down into oblivion.

The rest of the spring and early summer of 1918 saw Jack still attached to The Norfolk Regiment but without a command. The war was still in full flow on the Western Front but Jack had perhaps blotted his copy book once too many times for The War Office to be convinced that Jack should be sent back to the front and given another battalion command. This was not to happen at this moment although Jack would command one more battalion before his military career ended.

Somehow during April 1918 Jack came into contact with General Botha, an old friend from South Africa and now Prime Minister of The Union of South Africa. It is very likely that the South African press, whether pro British or nationalist, had been reporting on Jack's heroic exploits and, given that he had been back to South Africa in 1916, he was invited back again - according to Jack in a letter written later in February 1920 when he was resident at the Hotel Rubens "I undertook a recruiting tour at the request of the late General Botha" (Botha having died in August 1919). Botha had apparently offered to fund Jack's journey and whilst he was touring Jack also met General JMB Hertzog, leader of the pro nationalist party - and they got on well - perhaps too well for the British section in South Africa. As we know, Jack seemed to have the gift of either finding conflict and getting involved or where there was no conflict creating one. Touring the Eastern Cape, Jack arrived in East London in May 1918 in order to whip up more support for the war in France and swell the recruiting numbers - especially of Dutch South Africans being encouraged to go to France and rid their homeland of the Germans who had been there in occupation since 1914. Accordingly Jack seems to have at one and the same time got a taste for the stage and speech making but also managed to offend many of those listening. It is safe to say his early attempts at speech making were likely to be of the rabble rousing style and complaints were made to the British Consul. Such complaints about Kelly reached as far as Sierra Leone a few weeks later where Maj. General Thompson, then Commanding British Troops in West Africa, later made this observation back to the War Office:

"I think the Army Council should be in possession of the facts gathered by me in my recent visit to South Africa, that Lt. Colonel Kelly during his stay in South Africa more or less identified himself with the Nationalist party and with Mr Hertzogg in particular. He further made an injudicious speech at a recruiting meeting and altogether got into a bad odour with the English Section and I believe his leave was curtailed by Brigadier- General Martyn CMG who is now at home."

Maj.Gen.C.W.Thompson
12.2.1919   *(9)*

The most likely interpretation is that Jack with his new Victoria Cross and all his other medals, felt invulnerable, strong, potent and important. If we pause for a moment to consider what he had been through by the age of thirty-eight we can but wonder how he must have felt. He was still learning about life but had seen so much of death. He had wanted fame and fortune but now how to use it? He was back on a stage that he recognized and where he was now special - he was very likely one of the most decorated South Africans in the whole country and he had been invited to stand up tall, show his chest and he was ready to do it. Unfortunately Jack was, at this time, out of his depth when it came to making speeches and a novice in the sensitivities and balances of South African politics. In order to be successful, Jack probably said what he thought would win the day and gather the most positive reaction. It was only later that he realized what he had done and had to back track as Brigadier Martyn later wrote from his home in Exmouth in March 1919:

"Kelly apparently made some injudicious remarks in his addresses. I saw the account of one in the local press - and at once communicated with him referring to the instructions in the K.R., with reference to soldiers mixing themselves up in political meetings etc. He then returned to Cape Town and spoke to him on the matter. He assured me that he had not meant politics by any remark he had made, and after considerable conversation I was quite satisfied that his remarks were made in the excitement of the moment and that his educational attainments in my opinion did not suit him to making speeches, as he made statements which he considers harmless and not political which in a country like South Africa are at once seized on by the opposite political parties and turned to their own advantage. Lieut. Col. Kelly was, he informed me, a friend of Gen. Hertzog before the war and he certainly was on good terms with him on their visit to South Africa."

Having been admonished we might expect Jack yet again to have run up against authority but we discover that it was all about how he was handled. General Martyn clearly had a gentle but firm and non judgmental approach and this worked with Jack which resulted in the following epilogue from the General:

"No more loyal or gallant officer in my opinion is serving in H.M. Army, but also in my opinion he is not suitable for "speech making" in a country like South Africa and if I had been asked I should have said so. After the East London meeting and my telegram referred to above, Lieut. Col. Kelly came to Cape Town and I was fortunately able to get him a passage at once to England...."

Having extricated and learnt from this experience, a gentle trip home in the sun might have been wise but it was not to be. Leaving Capetown on 6th June 1918, Jack was, perhaps ill advisedly, put in command of the newly recruited South African troops on board H.M.S. *"City of Karachi"*. En route Jack, perhaps with that newly inflated ego that had already taken over, fell out explosively with the troops on board. Whether or not it was the VC or whether Jack really was something of a martinet - a real paradox if there ever was one, Jack apparently called the troops on board "damned South Africans" with bad discipline. One example of this was a reported case of a young Lieutenant caught by Jack with an NCO in his cabin smoking. Jack saw this as a dreadful breach of discipline and the mark of "an undisciplined rabble". Arriving in Sierra Leone, another Major General had another Kelly inspired mess to sort out and Major General Thompson had to call an enquiry into complaints wired over by a Lieutenant Baxter and a Major King. At the end of the hearing the General recorded:

"...although I did not suppose an entente cordiale was established yet I was fully under the impression that the matter was settled, that all parties were satisfied and that no further trouble would arise on the voyage."

The matter rumbled on for months as the South African High Commissioner demanded the War Office take further action. However in the best British tradition time marched on and it was not until March 1919 that a Horse Guards minute recorded:

"I think it is clear that Lieut. Col. Kelly is an officer whose tact is not on a par with his gallantry and I have no doubt he used forcible language. I suggest he should be so informed (the censure being of a mild description) and the High Commissioner be told that suitable action has been taken." (10)

141

This prophetic judgment on Jack's character was apt beyond belief as within four months of this being written, Jack had left to fight in northern Russia, fallen foul of the entire High Command there and was locking horns with Winston Churchill in a very gallant stand completely lacking in any form of tact.

(1)   Proceedings of divorce April 1919

(2)   Ibid

(3)   'The History of The Royal Inniskilling Fusilers'
         pp.84,111,112,113,118,226,288. From The National Army Museum
         Nummis Files

(4)   Liddell Hart, B.H. 'History of the First World War' p.440-441

(5)   Regimental Diary 1/Inniskillings p.84 and 111-113

(6)   Browne Capt. D.G, "The Tank in Action". (Blackwood, 1920)

(7)   Ibid p.226-228

(8)   The London Gazette, 11th January, 1918

(9)   National Archives, Kew

(10)   National Archives, Kew

CHAPTER SEVEN - PART ONE

'The habit of gambling contrary to reasonable calculations is a military vice which, as the pages of history reveal, has ruined more armies than any other cause.
- Captain Sir Basil Liddle Hart, 1944.

THE RUSSIAN REVOLUTION, 1917-1919

Although 1917 was another year of costly failure for all sides on The Western Front, it was also the year that paradoxically signalled the beginning of the end of the war. This was due to two major events of great political and military significance - the entry of the USA into the war and the fall of Russia in revolution.

In April 1917 the United States of America entered the war on the allied side. After a painful and long hesitation the military and economic might of the United States was to prove decisive. It would take some months for the men and materiel to reach the muddy battlefields of France but the German High Command recognized the inevitability of their fate unless the war could be won in France quickly. Hence they looked east to Russia.

From the very start of the war in 1914, the allies relied on splitting the German and Austrian armies over two fronts. After all it was the Tsar who had escalated the chance of conflict in his demands over Serbian neutrality and so it was only right that he put his armies into the field in the east to play their part while the British and French acted to protect Belgium. After initial successes, the Russian armies were beaten by Hindenburg and Ludendorf's attacks in early 1915. As the war went on through 1916 and into 1917 hardships and privations in Russia increased and the dangers of internal collapse grew. Although able to place six million men in the field at the start of the war, many of these men were poorly equipped and even more poorly fed. Ineffective command and poor supplies created mutiny both amongst the army and the navy during the winter of 1917 and the communist soviets fed on this discontent. The Tsar became ever more distant and unable to control events nor did he fully appreciate and understand the new social movements growing in the urban cities. The growth of socialism was not just new to Russia. The new political power that came with the need for labour created a new working class with its own political agenda and ambitions. The European brotherhood of socialism may have been new but it was there and events in Russia became the focus of attention for British politicians every bit as much as the fate of their armies in France. One politician watched with more horror than most - Winston Churchill.

The first serious disturbances began in January 1917. While Jack Kelly was at home in Cranley Gardens nursing his chest wound, Moscow and Petrograd fell under the weight of sustained Bolshevik unrest and blood ran in the streets. By March 1917 the riots had spread and the local authorities ran for their lives as the troops they had sent to crush the soviets joined them instead. Finding loyal troops and generals was now a harsh fact of life for the White or Royal and loyal Russians.

All the allied powers felt the same: alarm at the loss of Russia from the war effort and equal alarm that revolution might spread to their own workers and encourage supporters of communism and Bolshevism. It was clear that the rise of labour brought about by industrialisation was changing the political landscape but it was also evident that the explosion in Russia was due to the economic hardships of four years of war. It might not have been as bad in Britain but it was still bad. Food shortages, long casualty lists, anger at the authority and incompetence of the establishment, disintegrating morale and the growing militancy of the unions and labour party all raised the spectre of social unrest at home before the Germans could be defeated. Was the British monarchy under threat too? Opinions were divided in the cabinet led by Lloyd George, who had succeeded Asquith as Prime Minister in 1916 - having defected from the Liberal party along with many supporters. The truth was that no one really knew at this stage what was going on in Russia and who was loyal and what the Tsar could do to re establish his authority.

There was nothing new in the threat of Bolshevism in Russia. Europe had watched as revolution broke out in 1905 - and done nothing. What were they going to do now? In March 1917 it was clear that the Tsar had been deposed and chaos set in across this vast nation. The best form of information came from British businessmen and the many roving 'missions' that we had in Russia - a cover for open spying. Many large stocks were held in Russia and British investment in coal, wood and other raw materials was significant hence businessmen made a lot of noise and asked what was to be done. The moral dilemma for the British government and our own royal family was what to do to help Tsar Nicholas, his wife the Tsarina and their family. Could they be rescued, could they be bought by ransom? Could they be released by diplomatic means? The answer was undoubtedly yes on all three counts, so which did the British government try?

There were experts on the situation in Russia. As Robert Jackson pointed out men such as Colonel Alfred Knox (later General Knox) had informed the British government as early as 1914 that the Russian army could collapse at any time. (1) His views were rated very highly by many including Winston Churchill whose eyes were always clearly focused on the socialist menace both at home and abroad. Whenever possible, Churchill had used his position as First Lord of The Admiralty to send ammunition, guns and supplies to northern Russia to help support the Tsar and his armies - a massive liability now sitting in north Russia if they should fall into the wrong hands. R.H.Bruce Lockhart was another roving emissary to the Tsar and warned in 1915 and 1916 of the way events were turning. Thus it might be supposed that we had a plan to support the Tsar, our own King George V's cousin and loyal friend of this nation. More recently however new research has shown a gradual distancing of Britain, her government and her King from support for Tsar Nicholas. The King knew full well what was happening:

March 13th 1917:

Bad news from Russia, practically a revolution has broken out in Petrograd and some of the Guards regiments have mutinied against their officers. This rising is against the government and not the Tsar.
                              George V Diary (Kenneth Rose)

Trotsky stated it more clearly when he said that 'Neither at the front nor in the rear was there to be found a Brigade or a regiment ready to fight for Nicholas II'. (2)

After an initial period of shock, the British government seemed to drift in different directions about what could and should be done. The issues over entanglement in the affairs of another nation raised their ugly head and indecision and division developed here so Communism had a chance to grow and establish itself unchecked by intervention from the allies. George V continued to offer moral support his cousin and clear his own conscience as he wrote in a telegram to Nicholas on March 19th:

'Events of last week have deeply distressed me. My thoughts are constantly with you and I shall remain your true and devoted friend as you know I have been in the past.'

Nicholas never received this or any other telegram ever again from George V not because they were intercepted by Bolshevik guards or because the location of the Tsar was unknown but because it was stopped by Lloyd George. (3) By degrees, Lloyd George had come into the fold of the non interventionists in the cabinet, those who also saw a certain justice in what was happening in Russia:

'...the revolution whereby the Russian people have placed their destinies on the sure foundation of freedom is the greatest service which they have yet made to the cause for which the allied peoples have been fighting since 1914. It reveals the fundamental truth that this war is at bottom a struggle for Popular Government as for liberty.' (4)

In this short sentence we see some of the mastery of Lloyd George the Welsh wizard. At a stroke support for the Tsar was jettisoned, a play for the support for the votes of the new British working class was made in an attempt to bring them closer to the Liberal Party of which he was the leader and finally an overture to what would become the new masters of Russia was made. The Tsar was alone as far as Britain was concerned - although not quite. There were others in the coalition cabinet who were appalled at such sentiments. Some saw Bolshevism as a threat to all democracies not the saviour.

Churchill was not alone in wanting to strangle Bolshevism at birth but how to outmanouvre the Prime Minister and the wrath of the socialist movement in this country? That was the problem now. Lloyd George would stick to his dictate that *"It was not our duty to settle the political order of Russia."* (5)

Even more surprising than the government's desertion of the Tsar was the fact that George V also withdrew from an active policy of trying to save his cousin. Recent research has now established that during the spring and early summer of 1917 a series of high level meetings were held to discuss the Tsar's future. Although an ally, a relation of the British royal family and a staunch friend of Britain the decision that was taken was to distance British interests from the internal affairs of Russia - despite the protests of Churchill and others. The plan to send a warship to collect the Tsar and his family - discussed with Kerensky the then more moderate leader of the Provisional Government, was shelved even though Kerensky would have been glad to have been rid of the Tsar. A series of increasingly pointed and sharp letters were exchanged between Stamfordham, the King's Private Secretary, Balfour, the British Foreign Secretary and Sir George Buchanan the British Representative in Petrograd. It is clear than over these weeks George V became completely opposed to saving Nicholas and his family. Phrases such as "concern at the dangers of the voyage" (as if this were more dangerous than being placed in the hands of the Bolsheviks!), and "general grounds of expediency" betray the search for any moral excuse whatsoever for condemning Nicholas to his death.

Explanations of this complete volte face have also become clearer as historians uncover more archival evidence and place them against the political and social backcloth of the time. There was for example a real threat of socialist unrest growing in Britain in 1917. The strike rate was increasing and dissatisfaction with the war, the losses and the shortages aided this. How would the public react to the arrival of the Tsar and his family, saved from the clutches of the Russian working classes by the government? In addition the Royal Family, as now and as always, was acutely aware of the need to manage its own PR campaign very carefully. Avoiding placing the royal family in the public eye for the wrong reasons but at the same time maintaining the lustre of monarchy and divine rights has always been the balancing act waged as a private strategy against public opinion. A classic move on July 17th 1917 was formally to change the name of the royal family from Hanover to Windsor - without the war, the changing attitude of the public towards all things German and increasing alarm at attacks from 'radicals and extremists' this would never have happened. At the same time the Battenberg's changed their family name to Mountbatten and the new socialist menace had established itself as a real threat in the psyche of the establishment and political classes. Left isolated and marooned by all the allied powers the Tsar and his young and beautiful family were doomed and what has often been referred to as "this shabby affair" even surprised and shocked the Russians:

"With tears in his eyes scarcely able to control his emotions Sir George (Buchanan) informed the Russian Minister of Foreign Affairs of the British Governments final refusal to give refuge to the former Emperor of Russia…I can say definitely that this refusal was due exclusively to considerations of internal British politics." (6)

And so it was that the *"true and devoted friend"* that was George V deserted Nicholas in the face of threats to his own position from his own people. We will never know what Nicholas told his family. In

1992 the bodies of Nicholas and his family did actually reach Britain but only for forensic examination to determine in what order they were shot, had their bodies cut up, dumped in acid and buried and Lloyd George would no doubt have stood by his words that this was a moral price worth paying for in the struggle for 'popular liberty' in Russia.

The story did not quite end there as after the war, and partly due to Jack Kelly's developing role in highlighting British policy in Russia, storms of denial over the role of Britain in the murder of the Tsar followed. One such aspect involved Merial Buchanan, daughter of Sir George, who, after his death, stated that her father had falsified his memoirs to protect the King's honour - and to save his pension which Lloyd George had threatened would be stopped if he told the truth.

Thus it is clear that not only were there divisions on the Russian question at the highest levels within the cabinet of Lloyd George, there were also men who would stop at nothing to prevent Britain's involvement. Certainly Lloyd George would have none of it and so step forward men who were used to making decisions that were unpopular and often wrong - Winston Churchill and Lt. Col. Jack Sherwood Kelly VC, CMG, DSO.

At almost the same time as General Byng was formulating the finishing touches for the Third Army's role in the attack on Cambrai in October 1917, the Russian Revolution was about to explode into a new and decisive phase. Up to this point the Bolsheviks had played a relatively minor part in national events. Successive provisional governments came and went but failed to make any real progress despite high ideals and promises. Others had on the other hand been biding their time and watching. Lenin could have been a student of Sun Tzu who, over two thousand years ago, said:

"I have heard of military operations that were clumsy but swift, but I have never seen one that was skilful and lasted a long time. It is never beneficial to a nation to have a military operation continue for a long time."   (7)

For Lenin the successful takeover of power by the Bolsheviks depended on timing. With groups all around central government posturing for control, the Bolsheviks were able to build their resources and support all over Russia and most importantly amongst the army and the navy. Like Hitler would do only ten years later, Lenin watched, planned and waited so that his campaign was swift and ruthless. In the eye of the storm was Kerensky trying to patch up what he could from the chaos around him and contain the revolutionary ferment:

"What do they expect of me?" He shouted at Raymond Robbins, an *American ostensibly working for the Red Cross but actually a member of the American Intelligence Service. "Half the time I'm forced to talk Western European Liberalism to satisfy the allies and the rest of the time I have to talk Russian Slavic Socialism to keep myself alive!"*   (8)

Kerensky was the first leader to feel the pressure of outside influence. Key to the allied interest in Russia was the question of whether they would maintain forces in the field against the German and Austro-Hungarian armies and a close second was what the various governments were going to do to safeguard western financial interests, loans and investments in Russia from the revolutionaries.

Allied prospects of victory were now assured once the Americans arrived in sufficient numbers but this depended on keeping the war on two fronts going. Lloyd George may have publicly denounced intervention in the hope that his high minded form of democratic liberalism would appeal to his known disaffected masses but the reality of course was that Britain had been intervening in the affairs of Russia ever since the Crimea.

Well before 1914 western businessmen had been investing substantial sums in what today would be called the emerging markets - Imperial or Tsarist Russia being one of the largest. As Michael Sayers and Albert Kahn pointed out as long ago as 1946, men such as Herbert Hoover had private interests in no fewer than eleven Russian oil companies and in 1912 he had joined with the British multi millionaire Leslie Urquhart to form three timber and mineral companies in the Urals and Siberia. (9) Growth was dramatic as production costs were so low. Russo-Asiatic shares rose from $16.25 in 1913 to $47.50 by 1914 alone and western banks owned shares in numerous coal and silver mines, railroads, oil refineries and oil fields all purchased at bargain basement prices from the economically crippled Tsarist regime - oil that today has created hundreds of billionaires. Like vultures over a body not quite dead, the western powers watched and waited for a weakness that would allow further advantage - either economic or political. During 1917 instructions went out to buy as many banks as possible. This high risk strategy could only have been explained by the fact that they hoped, via economic exploitation, to take control of the Russian state once the Tsarist regime had gone forever and the Bolshevik menace had been eliminated - what would be left would be their economic stranglehold over the entire nation:

"...if the Bolsheviks could now be ousted by military intervention, Britain would have virtual control of the entire economy of White Russia." (10)

During the remaining months of 1917 and on into 1918, Lloyd George monitored events and played his dangerous game of political roulette balancing the potential dangers and opportunities in handling the growing socialist movement in Britain with the equally dangerous game of supporting the supposed growth of liberty in Russia with a view to controlling the outcome to the huge economic advantage of British business - much of which supported his party. Thus non intervention in a political sense did not mean non intervention economically. Somewhere lost in this higher stakes game was the Tsar and his family whose future remained uncertain over the months ahead and through the winter of 1917-1918.

During the summer of 1917 the Russian Army disintegrated. It had never been a unified fighting force but rather an amalgam of widely differing standards of unit fattened by whole corps of ethnic troops swelling ranks by numbers not quality. With the propaganda of the Bolsheviks permeating every thought of the ordinary soldier confusion reigned and loyalties waned and a rapid disintegration left senior commanders either dead or having to rely on their reputation to keep the loyalty of their men. Men such as Kornilov, Brusilov and Russky stood firm and loyal troops gravitated to loyal commanders and continued the fight against the Germans - others deserted in their thousands and drifted into the arms of the Bolsheviks.

Throughout these days the Germans prospered, their divisions exploiting the holes that opened up in front of them. The depth of desperation of loyal officers even saw them attack the German lines alone and meet certain death. Lenin and his senior aides had been planning, watching, preparing and amassing their forces and by October Lenin judged that the time was right to strike and then ten days that shook the world began:

"Consolidate your keenest energy, save up your extra strength, keep your form concealed and your plans secret, being unfathomable to enemies, waiting for a vulnerable gap to advance upon." - Lenin.

After the overthrow of Kerensky, Lenin immediately moved to end the war with Germany ordering General Dukhonin to begin negotiations for an armistice - he refused and was later shot. But talks did begin at Brest Litovsk in December 1917 and suddenly the worst fears of the allied powers became reality - they were no longer talking to Kerensky but to Lenin and his Soviets and the question now was what to do. If Lloyd George thought for a moment that his support for 'popular democracy' would be a vote winner with the Bolsheviks in power he was wrong. He now had the reaction of the British right, business and the conservative middle class to deal with. Direct military intervention was not possible. There were no spare troops in the Spring of 1918 and the German final offensive of the war was coming. Only the Americans or possibly the ever watchful Japanese could help and thus the policy of defensive intervention began to develop. Lenin played his own double and triple games. He knew that the longer the Germans could keep up the fight the more time he would have to win his own and establish the revolution permanently in Russia. The negotiations at Brest Litovsk therefore dragged on with the Germans becoming more impatient by the day. It also soon became evident that a further problem was looming. Both the allied powers, and especially Britain, had been helping Russia to stay in the war by sending huge amounts of guns, ammunition and stores to key Russian ports. In the Far East Japan now moved to recover these from Valdivostok. The British however chose to await events and left their vast caches in Archangel intact for now.

As Jack Sherwood Kelly walked out of Buckingham Palace on that cold misty London morning in January 1918, in another world far away the forces opposed to Bolshevism in Russia began to concentrate in various parts of Russia to try to restore the monarchy and the old order. To the far south General Kaledin deployed his loyal forces in the River Don and the British government now had to work out which side they were on. According to Robert Jackson this was not a decision to make now, instead in traditional and well practiced diplomatic style, the government supported both. As Bruce Lockhart recalled later:

"On New Year's Day (1918) I was back at the offices of the War Cabinet. A scheme was being evolved. It was certain that I was to return to Russia almost at once. In what capacity I was not told. Three days later all my doubts were put at rest. I was to go to Russia as head of a special mission to establish unofficial relations with the Bolsheviks…. My instructions were of the vaguest. I was to have no authority. If the Bolsheviks would give me the necessary diplomatic privileges without being recognized by the British government we would make a similar concession to Litvinoff whom the Bolsheviks had already appointed Soviet Ambassador in London." (11)

As Jack Kelly contemplated his future in that London spring of 1918, Lloyd George was also wondering how to survive the year and battled to use his wizard powers to the full to satisfy everyone. A few hundred miles to the west the Germans had also done their own pondering but they were now on the move and finally lost their patience with Lenin and struck out in major offensives in northern Russia. Within weeks the Bolsheviks had crumbled. Humiliating negotiation followed to buy the Germans off and huge swathes of Russian territory were ceded to the Germans and on March 3rd the Treaty of Brest Litovsk was finally signed. The Germans not over bothered about the legitimacy of those signing on behalf of the Russian people - had already decided that it mattered not whether it was a Russian Communist or a member of the Russian royal family that signed as long as someone did. Immediately after, the German divisions on the Eastern Front received their marching orders to head west and Ludendorf's 'fredensturm' offensive began on the Western front on March 21st 1918.

Under pressure all along the front to absorb these final and desperate German attacks it is not surprising that the Bolsheviks now tried to take advantage of allied distraction. Suddenly the massive stores in the north Russian ports became one of the keys to the success of the revolution as Lenin could arm his revolutionary guards and soviets with fresh guns and ammunition in endless supply. Rear Admiral Kemp was in command of the small British presence around Murmansk and was responsible for protecting convoys entering or leaving Murmansk. On 13th February 1918 he had already asked for a force of 6,000 men to guard the stores and warehouses which were being progressively looted by the local soviets. He could not afford to fire a shot for fear of sparking an incident on Russian soil. His request was denied but he did land 130 Royal Marines from his ships to reinforce the local Tsarist troops still loyal. In Britain this news began to permeate into the newspapers. The Foreign Office was of course, on the surface, appalled while the First lord of the Admiralty Sir Eric Geddes was supportive. General Knox went much futher and

THE RUSSIAN REVOLUTION, 1917-1919

called for 5,000 men to defend Murmansk and 15,000 men for Archangel. (12)   Such calls were not new as Brinkley points out:

'...an allied conference met in Paris on December 22nd 1917 to consider a special memorandum by The British Foreign Office. This memorandum, formulated largely by Lord Milner, stressed the necessity of keeping the Eastern Front active by every means possible...it recommended especially the further development of relations with General Alekseev and the Don Cossacks but also suggested the need for a more active allied policy in the Ukraine.' (13)

As an aside to all this we can note that Alfred Milner, who had been such a significant figure in South Africa during The Boer War and whose actions impacted on the life of Jack Kelly, was still very active and very much a part of the support for Lloyd George - and was again about to influence the life of Jack Kelly and others - as they were pawns in a great game played in the corridors of power. Thus on the surface Lloyd George preached non intervention and support for 'popular democracy' (whatever that meant in Russia at that time or any time) while behind the scenes tremendous pressure built for increased action to either support the loyal White Armies in crushing the Bolsheviks and thus preserving our economic interests in Russia or the complete opposite of working with the Bolsheviks depending on how events unfolded. A great game indeed where the lives of men were simply useful in achieving a political not moral end. According to Sayers and Kahn, Sir Samuel Hoare, Chief of the British Intelligence Service in Russia, had already recommended that the British and French governments back a coup led by General Kornilov that would at once *"keep Russia in the war, suppress the revolution and protect Anglo-French financial stakes in Russia."* (14)

Nor could Lloyd George complain that he was not extremely well informed about events in Russia. In early 1918, Captain S.G.Reilly had arrived in Russia as a member of the British Secret Service. He worked with and extended the spy rings across Russia and could boast '...sealed Red Army orders were being read in London before they were being opened in Moscow' - Reilly was also able to draw on large sums of money to finance his operations. Quite clearly had he and his closest advisors wanted to, Lloyd George could have extinguished the Bolshevik threat as Churchill had wanted to do - 'at birth'. As he played with the fate of millions and indeed to an extent the world, Lloyd George could see three distinct results in Russia. Firstly with mass peasant support (possibly armed with British stores in the north), increasing organization and bloodthirsty executions, Lenin was on the verge of winning complete power. This would lead to the destruction of capitalism and democracy inside Russia as a precursor to extending communism outside Russia. Secondly it was possible that Russia, as happened in the 1980s, could simply disintegrate. Already in 1917 and 1918 a number of areas had declared their independence. Lastly the allies could actively and openly support the loyal army commanders and divisions spread across Russia, release arms to them and even send allied troops to challenge and ultimately crush the passionate but ill equipped Bolshevik units.

Writing in the 1930s Lloyd George was clear that British aims were simple and always had been. These were to *'prevent military stores at Murmansk, Archangel and Vladivostok falling into enemy hands and to succour the Czech-Slovak troops in the Urals and enable them to reconstitute an anti-German front ...or to withdraw safely and join the allied forces in the west.'* (15)

Unfortunately for Lloyd George his attempts at sanitising both the degree of already extant British involvement and intervention, as he waited to see which side would win, or his efforts to minimize his aims were unconvincing to the judgment of history. Writing in 1958 E.M.Halliday in his excellent book 'The Ignorant Armies' (which Jack Kelly was soon to join) saw the agreement to occupy the northern ports of Russia as the preliminary to bridgeheads for a campaign of action. Any commander fighting a war on foreign soil needs bridgeheads and normally they have to be gained at tremendous cost in lives but the allies had three massive ports already in their hands should they decide to use them. These ports also had all the stores needed to support an entire Army if it were landed. Halliday went much further in identifying more penetrating and sinister motives:

'...one of them officially admitted, the other was officially concealed - although it was widely known to exist. The first was a desire to strike down through north Russia from Archangel to the Trans-Siberian railroad, 400 miles to the south and there effect a junction with the Czechs , who in the meantime were to have fought their way westward along that railroad until they reached at least as far as the City of Viatka. This would have posed a new and formidable allied threat to Germany in the East. The second was the hope that this manoeuver, or military events subsequent to it, might happily coincide with a complete overthrow of the communist government, thus removing a nasty threat to world security and to civilization.' (16)

Around Lloyd George and behind closed doors there was no sympathy for 'popular democracy' or respect for the Bolsheviks. To many this was simply political rubbish designed to keep Lloyd

George, his party and his cronies in power. Indeed one of the cabinet's closest advisors General Knox had already suggested at least five hundred men be sent to Archangel and in a 1917 conversation his longer term motives were clear :

Knox: "I am not interested in stabilizing Kerensky and his government. It is incompetent and inefficient and worthless."

Robbins: "Well General, you were with Korninlov."

Knox: (In great anger and shouting) "The only thing in Russia today is a military dictatorship. These people have got to have the whip hand over them!"

Robbins: "General, you may get a dictatorship of a very different character."

Knox: "You mean this Trotsky-Lenin-Bolshevik stuff - this soap box stuff?"

Robbins: "Yes, that is what I mean."

Knox: "Robbins, you are not a military man. You do not know anything about military affairs. Military men know what to do with this kind of stuff. We stand them up and shoot them!"   (17)

So not much ambiguity there about what Knox and no doubt many if not the majority including Churchill felt needed to be done in Russia. With the volunteer and loyal army of Denekin to the south, the Czech and Slovak armies to the west and a strong allied force in the north (at least the size of a division) it was at this moment apparently possible to snuff out the Bolshevik Revolution as soon as the war in the west had been won. The key problem was how to get Lloyd George to support this strategy and how to unite both the cabinet and British public behind the scheme.

(1)   'At War with the Bolsheviks', Robert Jackson. (Tom Stacey, 1972) p.18-21

(2)   'World War One', Basil Liddle Hart, Ch.5 p.180

(3)   'The File on the Tsar' by A. Summers and T. Mangold. (Harper & Row) p.244

(4)   Lloyd George to Prince Lvov quoted in Rose pp.209-210

(5)   'The War Memoirs of David Lloyd George' (Odhams Press) Vol. II, p.1888

(6)   Rose Ibid p.211

(7)   'The Art of War' by Sun Tzu , translated by Thomas Cleary (Shambhala, 2003) p.59

(8)   'The Great Conspiracy Against Russia' by Michael Sayers and
        Albert Kahn.   (Boni & Gaer, 1946), p.3

(9)   ibid pp.35-37

(10)   'The Road to Intervention, March - November 1918' by M. Kettle.
        (Routledge, 1988)

(11)   'Lockhart. British Agent. Quoted in Jackson p.29-30

(12)   Jackson pp.36-37

(13)   'The Volunteer Army & Allied Intervention in South Russia, 1917-1921'
        by G.A.Brinkley. (Notre Dame Press, 1966) p.28

(14)   Sayers & Kahn p.3

(15)   'Memoirs', Lloyd George, p.1891

(16)   'The Ignorant Armies' by E.M.Halliday (Weidenfeld & Nichoilson,
        1958). pp.15-25

CHAPTER SEVEN - PART TWO

'In a minute there can be many days'.
                - William Shakespere, Romeo and Juliet

INTERVENTION AND COURT MARTIAL, 1919

Throughout the Spring and Summer of 1918, Jack was posted back to Suffolk where during the week he was again back training new volunteers coming through what was now the ranks of the 12th Service Battalion of the Norfolks. After all the heady days of Gallipoli, DSOs, the adulation of his countrymen in South Africa and fighting on the Somme culminating in his Victoria Cross, this was almost too much to bear. The last four years had given Jack a reason for existence, a cause, a whole social network, rank, authority, respect, excitement, glory and challenge. It had also given him a wife and a home amongst one of the most respected families in London. However, he would have preferred to face yet more German bullets, gas and the hell of the Somme than take the weekly train to Bury St Edmunds and the mundane routine of a Training Major for recruits. Every day became a struggle and every hour was a reminder of his inactivity in stark contrast to the adulation of previous months.

Just as it had been in 1902 and again in 1906, Jack was at war with himself, hard if not impossible to live with, fractious, frustrated and explosive. Not surprisingly his relationship with Nellie continued to suffer. When he was fighting and on leave he was predictable and jovial, fun and good company. Almost a template of "Paddy" Blair Mayne of the SAS in World War II, when he was away from conflict with nothing to do or feeling unwanted Jack was unpredictable. He had dramatic changes of mood and his temper was no respecter of people or rank. After the VC celebrations in January 1918, and even though the two of them were featured in The Ladies Field in April 1918 as the epitome of style and marital bliss, by the autumn it was clear that Jack had had enough of his marriage and within a year Nellie would be forced into filing for a divorce from a man she adored. It may have been that he wanted their relationship to work. We can surmise this because later in life Jack did indeed want Nellie in his life to lean on but for now he could not see or feel that. His sense of indestructibility was so strong that he could not see the need for anyone alongside him and his beleaguered state of mind meant that no-one could get near to him emotionally. Was this the result of his tragic and traumatic experiences as a child when he lost his mother and twin brother? Had he been fighting battles with himself and everyone else ever since? Did he ever grieve - did he know how to grieve and was he scared of nothing except giving way to his emotions with someone who then might let him down? Modern psychology teaches us that men especially become driven in order to both feel valued but also to vent a rage that they cannot control in any other way. They become disinterested in what may happen to them and have nothing except anger to drive them along. Couple this with an Irish temperament where to argue is sometimes almost the sole reason for existence, and we have a deep and complex man difficult to love but who also did not know how to love either himself or others.

Meanwhile events in Russia began to take centre stage over events on The Western Front. In April 1918 the Tsar and his family had been moved from Siberia where they had been held captive for the previous six months to Ekaterinburg in The Ural Mountains. This remote place was to become their cemetery as on July 17th the Tsar and his beautiful family were shot, bayoneted, burned in sulphuric acid and buried. The Tsarist regime had ended.

Lt.Col. Sherwood Kelly V.C. outside the gates of Buckingham Palace on 23rd October 1918. Pictured here from the left are Nellie (with hat and furs), brother Clifford and Oswald, Jack's younger brother (above the medal).

Jack (standing centre) on board "Kelly's Mystery Ships" - North Russia, Summer 1919 with 2nd. Bn. The Hampshire Regiment.

6 V.C. winners on board The S.S.
Stephen en route to Archangel,
May 1919.

Back row:
Lt.Col. D.G. Johnson V.C., D.S.O., M.C.,
The South Wales Borderers.
Brig.Gen. G.W. St. George Grogan
V.C., C.M.G., D.S.O. and Bar,
The Worcestershire Regt.
Lt.Col. Jack Sherwood Kelly
V.C., C.M.G., D.S.O.
Capt. A.C.T. White V.C., M.C.,
The Yorkshire Regt.
Front sitting:
Lt. M.S.S. Moore V.C.
The Hampshire Regt.
Lt. A.M. Toye V.C., M.C.,
The Middlesex Regt.

*The front
page of
The Daily
Express,
Saturday
13th
September
1919*

A grim faced Lt. Col. Jack Sherwood Kelly V.C., C.M.G., D.S.O., still in the uniform of The Hampshire Regiment on his way to his court martial at Middlesex Guildhall, 28th October 1919, a little over a year after having received his Victoria Cross in the same month in 1918.

Jack's V.C., C.M.G., D.S.O. and group to be found in the Johannesburg Museum of Military History, South Africa. Although mounted in the wrong order they are an undoubted record of service to his country.

Nellie Sherwood Kelly as featured in 'The Ladies Field,' April 1918 - courtesy of The National Newspaper Library.

The last photograph of Jack taken around 1928 aged 48 - courtesy of The National Portrait Gallery, London.

Over the next few months the Bolsheviks murdered tens of thousands more and their Red Army divisions began to take shape and become increasingly formidable. Such a strengthening of the Bolshevik grip over Russia did not go unnoticed and during May 1918 Major Gen. F.C.Poole was appointed as Commander of British forces in northern Russia and 560 men were dispatched to Archangel and 600 men to Murmansk to guard and defend the stores there and prevent them from falling into Bolshevik hands. Trotsky was enraged by these actions which to him looked like an invasion of Russian territory and Red Army units surrounded, as best they could, the ports. French and American troops were also earmarked to defend stores in the east - like vultures waiting for the Russian Bolshevik bear to fall and be devoured by Western Imperialist ambitions. Any pretence that the British were in fact trying to work with the Bolsheviks was blown apart on 31st July 1918 when Admiral Kemp organized a coup in the city of Archangel expelling the Bolshevik Soviet in charge of the town. With the Tsarist Imperial flag flying over the town hall backed by the small but well equipped force a British bridgehead in Russia with enormous stockpiles of ammunition and guns was ready and waiting for either expansion into Russia or withdrawal. There was therefore already an active support from the British Army for the White Russians despite what Lloyd George might have protested.

General Poole had just over 2,000 men to guard an area six times the size of England. In November 1918 units of the Royal Sussex and Green Howard's Regiments also arrived in Murmansk just in time to experience the severities of a Russian winter. Huge snow drifts, average temperatures of -30 degrees centigrade and constant patrolling deep into Bolshevik territory took their toll. On the surface these small numbers of reinforcements were being sent to guard the stores intended for the White Army troops now fighting for a dead regime. However, they were increasingly pushing inland, up to 350 miles probing and pushing at the Red Army which was not yet strong enough in the area to push back but the situation was changing and deteriorating on the ground. At the same time on November 11th 1918 that The Great War ended on the Western Front the Bolsheviks launched a massive attack on the Dvina River in north Russia against troops of A Company Royal Scots. A desperate action followed including a personal charge by Sergeant Salmons who:

'Charged into the middle of the enemy ranks, firing a Lewis gun from the hip until he collapsed, his body torn by bullets and bayonet thrusts, in the middle of a heap of dead and dying Bolsheviks.' (1)

After the attack had been beaten off 19 infantrymen of the Royal Scots had been killed and 34 wounded. Similar actions took place throughout the coming months with men who had recently survived The Great War.

The British troops now serving in the Murmansk area had reached sizeable proportions and had been divided into 236 and 237 Brigades commanded by Brigadiers Turner and Price respectively. In October a new Commander at Archangel had been appointed in Maj. Gen. Edmund Ironside. The 38 year old Ironside had been commanding a Brigade in France when he was hurriedly promoted and sent to Russia. In the Archangel sector however there were fewer regular British units although those that were there were being ordered deep into hostile territory largely advancing down the Dvina River. Apart from the conditions and shortages of supplies the Red Army was also increasingly flexing its muscles with heavy attacks in January in the Shenkursk region 400 miles to the south of Archangel. After the privations of the severe winter, numerous cases of frostbite and some desperate defensive actions the troops of Ironsides 'Elope' Force waited for a decision to be made on their future. Until then Ironside brought his units back into a defensive perimeter around Archangel. After all the war had, by February 1919, been over for more than 3 months and so the German threat to the supplies had been removed.

While the future was being pondered, Ironside was developing his own unique leadership style in Archangel. One incident is worthy of note. In early December a group of locally recruited men supposedly loyal to the Tsarist regime mutinied and barricaded themselves into a barracks block hoping to start a coup that would see the whole of Archangel rise up and throw the British out. It did not develop as they hoped and thirteen men were rounded up and court martialled by Ironside. They were sentenced to death and according to Ironside's later account of this and subsequent events at Archangel, they were reprieved and given life sentences. However more recent research suggested that they were in fact lined up and shot in the back of the neck - and Ironside signed the death warrants. Amongst other things this tells us that Ironside was happy to rewrite history in his attempts to sanitise events - vital after Lt.Col Jack Kelly arrived as part of his command.

Opinions over Russia were in turmoil and Lloyd George had done nothing to clarify a situation that he hoped to bend to his advantage whatever the outcome. One option now open to him had crystallized into a withdrawal of all troops immediately and the destruction of stores leaving the internal affairs of Russia left to Russia. After all, the German threat to the stores had gone so why remain? If Lloyd George really did want popular democracy to rule regardless of British strategic, economic or political interests then that was the obvious answer - but significant financial and business interests were at stake and, just as today, they dictated responses.

Alternatively the stores could be protected by a limited ring of defences until they could be handed over to White Russian units. This was supporting the old legitimacy of Russia and the forces encouraged by the British and French to fight Bolshevism. Men such as Balfour and Milner, always with an eye on the prize that fate might gift them, favoured this. In other words to continue to watch and wait whilst protecting the stores by force if needs be.

There was a third option that was being aggressively advocated by the new Secretary for War appointed in 1919 - Winston Churchill. Churchill had never disguised his hatred of Bolshevism. In April 1918 he had written about using Czech troops against the Bolsheviks not the Germans. Lenin to Churchill was like *'a plague bacillus'* with the *'foul baboonery of Bolshevism'* being something to be destroyed not watched while it festered and spread. In later life Churchill reflected that the Tsarist regime had almost survived *"With victory in her grasp she fell upon the earth, devoured alive, like Herod of old, by worms"*. Little doubt then about what Churchill advocated. In December 1918 he had demanded that *"the allies intervene thoroughly with large forces, abundantly supplied with mechanical devices"*. He was not alone but he did not have the support of the Prime Minister. However this was hardly necessary for someone like Churchill. Early on in his new role he sent out a 'Secret and Urgent' request for information from field commanders enquiring how they felt their men would react if they were ordered to fight in Russia against the Bolsheviks. Their response left no room for doubt - *"they would parade for service overseas with the exception of Russia"*. (2) In fact the situation was deteriorating as many units began to grumble as they waited to be allowed to return home. There were even mutinous signs from British regiments and the fear that Bolshevism was spreading like a virus with agitators already at work in Britain was a very real one. Therefore, if using well equipped and experienced troops was the best way of ensuring Bolshevism and therefore Communism was crushed Churchill would have to find them without ordering the army to do it directly.

In his perceptive study of Churchill, Rhodes James identifies some of his key characteristics that were evident back in 1914 and 1915 - a single minded determination to get a plan through despite the odds once his mind was made up - just like Jack Kelly. Churchill balanced an uncertain cabinet and an equally uncertain Prime Minister with consummate ease. He was a blustering warship on the surface, a silent torpedo under it. His opening salvoes in December 1918 of 'thorough intervention' and 'large forces' had been transformed into 'messages of defiance' and 'material support' by February 1919. He was working towards the same end but by different means. He was well aware that Lloyd George and indeed no party was now able to operate independently of the reaction of the new British labour movement. He may not have liked it but he could deal with it. Churchill's tactical appreciation of the political battlefield was impressive and as he played the moral servant of government on the one hand, he exploited the weaknesses he was creating on the other.

"The sooner he was informed of the Governments policy (on Russia) the sooner he could start the preliminary arrangements" (arrangements that of course were already under way).

Churchill could see that the cabinet was racked by indecision on what action to take but equally desperate for the communist revolution to fail:

"The downfall of Bolshevism was universally desired in the British cabinet. Ministers hoped that this could be achieved with British material assistance but without the need to intervene militarily."

Lloyd George was also away in France as he worked on the treaty being discussed at Versailles that would punish Germans and ensure that this had been the war to end all wars. Such absence coupled with indecision gave Churchill the openings he needed.

"In these conditions of drift and irresolution, the Prime Minister frequently absent and biding his time, there was a good opportunity for a single minded man to carry his views considerably further than would have been the case in more normal conditions." (3)

As Martin Gilbert has pointed out, Churchill may have had strong views about what needed to be done in Russia but he had not been in a position to do much about it of substance until 10th January 1919 when he was appointed Minister of War in Lloyd Georges newly elected government. The newspapers were already closely monitoring events and only the week before Churchill took up his new role The Daily Express commented:

"We are sorry for the Russians, but they must fight it out amongst themselves. Great Britain is already the policeman of half the world. It will not and cannot be the policeman of all Europe. We want to return to industry and to restore the ravages of war. We want to see our sons home again. In fact we want peace. The frozen plains of Eastern Europe are not worth the bones of a single British Grenadier." (4)

Completely unfased, during February and March 1919 Churchill worked tirelessly to achieve two objectives. On the one hand he wanted to convince his colleagues and the Prime Minister that

Britain must play a more active role in defeating Bolshevism without being seen to interfere in the internal affairs of Russia. On the other he had to find a way of increasing the military power of the British Army in northern Russia - without ordering the Army to do it. His solution was to call for volunteers to go to Russia as a Russian Relief Force to bring back the men already out there - and then order these new forces into the heartland of Russia and to Moscow itself. A bold, daring and dangerous plan but full of hope and dash which appealed to both those around him in power but also to the men who volunteered their goodwill and patriotism for a cause presented so brilliantly.

By January 1919, a little over a year after being photographed together outside Buckingham Palace, the marriage between Jack and Nellie seemed effectively over. Jack had moved from Nellie's beautiful home in South Kensington at Cranley Gardens and was living near Windsor. Later in 1922, Jack was to appear in court for non payment of his gas bill. He cited poverty as the reason which suggests that he and Nellie completely parted and he was left with no income - until they reunited again in 1923.

Left with probably little option by Jack, divorce proceedings had begun and in April 1919 the matter reached the newspapers. The famous VC hero of only a year before was now being cited as a difficult if not impossible man to live with for whom "the old fascinations" had returned within months of marriage - Nellie especially had found it acutely embarrassing on her trip to South Africa as we know. But she loved him and the turmoil must have been incredibly hard for her to bear. We can be reasonably sure that for Jack however the matter was a pretty open and shut case. Jack had never easily adjusted to married life, he was a free spirit and a quite selfish one who now had other things on his mind. The past year had been boring and dull, he had put on weight, he started drinking heavily and he was frustrated not to have a new command to go with his VC. Moreover it seems likely that he had been having an affair for some time. In the mass of papers relating to Jack held in The National Archives in Kew there is a short unassuming letter. Writing from Northern Russia on the same day he wrote to his friend in London complaining about events in Russia, Jack also wrote on 26th July to Mrs Cameron of Dunkerry Lodge in Somerset:

> *2nd Hampshire Regt.*
> *26th July, 1919*
>
> *Dear Old Girl,*
>
> *Your letter of the 9th inst received last evening - You could not have been in love with me when it was written - one of your hate moods - Eh ! Any way I am training myself to realize that you are never likely to wish to marry me - Wise Girl - Yes I received your other two letters - I envy you your freedom - anyway I hope soon to join those ranks - I am glad you like the plates etc. I sent you - I have eight films in all - I long to see my Babe, news of her acts as a tonic on me -*
>
> *- Jonnie*
>
> *OAS Mrs Cameron*
> *Dunkerry Lodge*
> *Minehead*
> *Somerset*
>
> *Give my Babe a huge hug and kiss from me - (5)*

This is not a letter written to a friend. Jack was clearly in conversation with a woman with whom he had discussed marriage previously and the two references to his "babe" are almost certainly in respect of a child. Indeed it may have been this relationship that triggered Nellie's decision to divorce Jack, although the specifics of his affair were not used in court for obvious reasons. It is some measure of his complete lack of real affection for Nellie that he wished to join the ranks of the "free" and clearly now had no interest in his marriage.

At the age of 39 he was still a young man but physically he had treated his body hard. The wounds on his frame hurt every day as did his chest from the effects of both gas in 1915 and the bullet wound of 1916. But he was perhaps at his prime of self confidence - not to say arrogance and selfish determination to fight. He was an Ulsterman and we can safely appreciate that he would not shrink from a fight. If there was not one going on that he could join then he would create one. If there was no argument taking place then he would argue about why not and if we are in any doubt about his bloody mindedness towards Nellie, one only needs to recognise that in the very same month that Nellie was going through the public agony of a divorce from a man whom she had idolized, the same man was already volunteering and preparing to travel to Russia as part of Churchill's 'Volunteer Relief Force' the very next month. Not for him quiet contemplation of the hurt he had caused and reflecting on the loss of such a kind and generous woman but packing his bags, cleaning his uniform and marching to a station to pick up where he had left off a year before. This is what Nellie meant by 'impossible' and for her the pain and tragedy of the emotional loss must have been deep. Also now to see the man she had kept alive offer himself for more war this time in Russia must have been devastating - as was no doubt news of his relationship with Mrs Cameron. One can only hope that her wide family and her strong brother were there to support her in what could only have been a heart breaking experience where Nellie felt her lonely days of the past were about to return and the man she loved was once more driving his way to glory.

Whatever happened in court we may not know but Jack did not even turn up to give evidence - he was already on board ship. Nellie, as far as we know, decided not to proceed. Maybe, just maybe, if he returned from Russia he would change...

Having been persuaded that formal and open action was impossible and that the army would not follow, Churchill pressed on with his reserve plan and thus has been judged by historians as the architect of intervention in Russia at this time. In possibly the most recent detailed book to be published on Churchill's role in this whole episode in 2006, Clifford Kinvig states unequivocally that:

"Despite tremendous losses in World War One, a considerable force landed in Russia in 1918/1919 under the auspices of Winston Churchill. The aim was to influence the military and political outcome of the Russian Revolution." (6)

Lloyd George knew full well that Churchill wanted a full scale war against the Bolsheviks but could not have his way. Lloyd George was also well aware of Churchill's already highly suspect reputation as a man who would rashly support potentially disastrous military enterprises as both Antwerp and Gallipoli had shown - and Norway in 1940 would show again. The debate dogged cabinet discussions until March 4th 1919 when at last the decision was taken to evacuate all British troops from Northern Russia by June. For Churchill this was a disaster. Not at all used to not having his own way and convinced that this decision was wrong Churchill swung into action with the idea of sending out a relief force even larger than the one that was already out there to bring it back ! While they were there of course, it might be possible to either provoke a war or even get as far as Moscow and overthrow the Bolsheviks - as Minister of War he was in the key position to force the pace and issue orders to the commanders that he had appointed. Churchill was playing a dangerous game but as Oscar Wilde once so aptly put it when he could have been referring to Churchill:

"In matters of grave importance, style not sincerity, is the vital thing." (7)

Thus a relief force of volunteers was called for with the aim of supporting the White Russian Army (or what was left of it) and bringing back the men from north Russia who had been out there alone for nearly a year. The tone was set for 'relief' and 'rescue' but the fact was to intervention by any other name. Churchill was no fool but neither were those who monitored his political career and, responding on the decision to evacuate all troops from Russia the Daily Express again warned:

"Even with this undertaking given by the government to do the sensible thing, we must watch Mr. Churchill carefully. There is too much of the warlord about him."

By January 1919 the general demobilization of the British Army was well under way and this applied to the battle hardened and weary 29th Division like any other. The KOSBs and 2nd Hampshires had met in a final football match just prior to arriving back in barracks in Aldershot and then seeing after a few weeks, the regiments and battalions break up forever. The War Office had decided to keep a small cadre of men from each regiment as training troops, as new recruits joined up and these were the most experienced and battle trained men from each battalion. The 2nd Hampshires soon received news of the situation in Russia. It was presented to the men as a new enterprise, driven by Churchill's persuasive energy, to support the weak and overstretched British units trying to guard both the munitions and to help the rightful government against the evil revolutionaries. Who would not be stirred by such propaganda as demonstrated by the Regimental Diary of the Hampshires:

"Operations had been continued to assist those 'White' Russians who were friendly to the Allies, but the troops originally sent out were mostly units of 'low category' men including many due for demobilization, and early in 1919 it was decided to relieve them with Regulars."

They of course had no idea of the reality of the situation they were travelling to. Ironside was attempting to hold lines that were over extended, he was reliant on his own troops whose morale was dropping by the day, many of whom were sympathetic to the cause of the working Russia Bolshevik and whose fighting quality was very variable and indeed were cited by Jack Kelly for their murder of a number of British officers. He was also using a hotch potch of other nationalities on whom they could not rely. At the same time it was not clear whether he was fighting to protect the stores or to help the White Russians in their war - the consequences were potentially disastrous as he wavered between the two not knowing whether he was supposed to be actively fighting the Bolsheviks alongside the White Russian units or simply holding the line until relieved and withdrawn. In fact Ironside had done a superb job in establishing a rapport with local leaders in a complex political situation with fear of collapse and confusion infecting every action and every day. Equally he had put a command together that was effective. What he did not have were clear orders as Churchill awaited events in Britain to see if circumstances could be changed to suit his purpose - the men in Russia therefore were just pawns in another of his politico/strategic games. The local Russians were by now of course dependent on the British and had put their faith in them for both protection and support. Churchill's speech in The House of Commons on March 3rd reached Ironside on March 8th and although it gave at least some clarity to Ironside that he was there for a good reason, the worlds of the soldier and the politician were still a universe apart. In a master stroke of wordsmith genius, Churchill was now seeking to build support for those who had put their trust in Britain - a superbly deft tactic to play on the conscience of the British press:

"Further, we have incurred heavy commitments towards the people of those districts who have espoused our cause, and to the Russian forces fighting with us. It has been the custom of this country to pay particular attention to matters of this kind and always to endeavor, the best of our ability, to do our duty by those who have put their trust in us and who have run into danger in consequence of action which we have advised them to take." (8)

At a stroke of a pen and a speech Churchill provided a cause for supportive forces to rally around and provided the potential for the relief force to also need to hold faith with those it had inspired to resist; although this had been entirely at odds with the known view of cabinet. On 25th April, Ironside received a package from Churchill. Interestingly in his memoirs Ironside admits that the package contained no orders - this even though at the cabinet meeting on 4th March an explicit decision had been made to withdraw. Ironside, perhaps trying to validate his part in history, stated that *"Though I was still left without instructions, I had now a better idea of what was going on in Russia and could see what was in the minds of The General Staff."* *(9)* Given that the package had come from Churchill, given that it was over six weeks since a decision had been made to withdraw, one is left to ask the question why were there no explicit orders on preparing to withdraw? Why was the commander in the field left to assume what he was to do? That is probably because there were no orders to withdraw because Churchill had not issued them. Instead he was hoping that there was still some way for the existing troops and the relief force about to arrive to be able to crush the Bolshevik revolution. It was all about timing. If Churchill could keep the existing army in the field and reinforce it with 8,000 fresh and experienced troops while the White Russians prepared for their Spring offensive then there was still a chance. If they withdrew then there was not but this could not be committed to paper. Even more deftly as only the surest of politicians would know how to do, responsibility for the increasingly offensive operations against the Bolsheviks would shift from Churchill and onto Ironside.

Thus for men to whom the Army was their life and fighting their reason for existence, possibly with no family to return to, this was a rescue operation to bring back British troops under threat, it was not an invasion. There were also those in the Army who hated what communism represented, it being the opposite of the 'popular democracy' that Lloyd George professed to be seeing unfold in Russia. By March Churchill had got his way. He had prepared the ground well and kept open the objectives of action - only one of which was to bring back the men stranded in Russia. Indeed deliberate ambiguity was a key ploy and Churchill had no problem in getting his volunteers. The public call for volunteers took place on

8th April and within hours over 60 men had signed up. Posters went up for the RRF and the newspapers carried patriotic reports of scenes in recruiting offices where men only just recently released from duty queued up in lines. As The Daily Mail reported:

'The fighting spirit of the old army is aflame. Yesterday hundreds of veterans of The Great War were crowding Great Scotland Yard, Whitehall (where Jack turned up that very day), to join the North Russian Relief Force.'

On the whole it was only senior men and officers who turned up - mostly career soldiers and with a long service history, ideal men for such a force. Jack Kelly also arrived having been following developments in the newspapers and in conversations with his pals in the bar at The Authors' Club where he spent many evenings. Of course the men were being lied to. They had no idea that they were actually being sent out to push the political and military situation into a favourable position for Churchill. Former officers who were now unemployed could now be found serving as Corporals and one naval officer noted when part of the relief force arrived *'They are all volunteers, and any quantity of ex-officers in the ranks, colonels etc galore ; fellows wearing DSO's and MC's in private's uniform. I have never seen a finer crowd of men anywhere.'* (10)

Within two weeks a force of 8,000 men had been recruited - double the size Churchill had expected and he took them all. Two brigades were formed under two explosive and relatively young Brigadiers - G.W.St George Grogan and L.W.deV Sadler -Jackson. What was to become the 2nd Hampshires was in fact an amalgam of men from many regular regiments. Although the Headquarters Company was made up of Hampshire's and there were officers from the regiment spread throughout, there were also volunteers from The Somerset Light Infantry, Dorset Regiment and Wiltshires and their Commanding Officer was to be none other than Lt. Col. Jack Sherwood Kelly VC, CMG, DSO. This was to be Jack's fifth and final regimental link - he had come a long way on his five year journey through the ranks of King Edward's Light Horse, The Norfolks, The KOSBs, the Inniskillings and now The Hampshires.

The battalion was attached to Grogan's Brigade and ordered to assemble at Crowbridge Barracks to the south of Tunbridge Wells in Kent where it had around two weeks to fit itself out, drill and get to know the Commanding Officer before it was moved in haste to Tilbury Docks by rail on 13th May. Thus another Churchill escapade was about to begin based more on his impetuosity than reality and with the customary lack of planning, direction, aim and support. Had the men been more aware of Antwerp and Gallipoli they might have realised this. Their ship, *The SS Stephen*, left that evening and travelled at speed through stormy grey, icy waters, and arrived outside Archangel on 21st May 1919.

The mood on board was by all accounts one full of excitement, noise and incident as the men who had come together felt rather special - they were after all volunteers and this gave rise to a certain amount of freedom in attitude. Whilst on board with his battalion there was an opportunity for Jack to meet old acquaintances and make new ones too. One remarkable photograph survives showing Jack on board his troop ship together with five fellow VC winners:

Lt. Col. D.G. Johnson VC, DSO, MC - The South Wales' Borderers.

Brigadier General G.W. St George Grogan VC, CMG, DSO and Bar - The Worcestershire Regiment.

Captain A.C.T White VC, MC - The Yorkshire Regiment.

Lt. M.Moore VC - The Hampshire Regiment.

Lt. A.M.Toye VC, MC - The Middlesex Regiment.

These men, who had already offered everything including their lives in the past four years, were now giving even more on this operation and there is a sense of missionary zeal in this particular group photograph and it is almost certain that they felt in the vanguard of something far greater that was unfolding. After all there was scarcely a need for six winners of the Victoria Cross to travel to Russia with a further 8,000 men to help the withdrawal of fewer than 3,000 men. Maybe they were not as ignorant as some historians would like to see them. Certainly Churchill must have been delighted when he saw the quality of men going to carry out his plan. While Lloyd George was clear that a military solution was not being employed, Churchill was doing exactly that. News was reaching London every day of the excesses of the Red Terror with assassinations, murders and executions commonplace. Churchill once told his constituents at Dundee:

"Civilization is being completely extinguished over gigantic areas, while Bolsheviks hop and caper like troops of ferocious baboons amid the ruins of cities and the corpses of their victims". Although one day he would sit alongside Stalin, he was never to change his views on the Bolsheviks.

On arrival the *SS Stephen* waited for some ice to clear before disembarking the troops. The Hampshires were attached to 238

Special Brigade to be commanded by Grogan himself. Unlike the Baltic Sea, northern Russia was just coming into a hot sticky, insect ridden Spring. Some days offered frost covered ground while others sticky mud as the countryside started to wake up after winter. The town and barracks were grey and sullen and there was an air of unease - the wider conflict in Russia was not that far away and getting closer every day. Commanders were quickly briefed on the situation, warned of the unreliability of supposedly loyal Russian troops and the known dispositions of the local Red Army Bolshevik forces surrounding them. Ironside admitted in his recollections of the events that *"the men and officers were all volunteers who had been specially chosen for their physical fitness and experience of fighting"* - that was certainly true of the Commanding Officer of the 2nd Hampshires. Early on Ironside had a taste of exactly what had arrived when he inspected The Hampshires:

"As I was talking to The Hampshires telling them what they were likely to meet and how important to destroy Bolshevism (!), I heard a sort of running commentary coming from behind me. "Good for you! That's the stuff to give them!" It came from the C.O. of the battalion. I signalled to him to stop with my hand. I thought that I was unconventional to stand anything, but this was more than I could tolerate. He was a man who had fought all through the late war with great distinction, rising from Lieutenant to Lieut. Colonel. He was not a regular officer but he had been specially chosen for his fighting experience. It was difficult to know how to deal with the incident. It takes all kinds to make a fighting army, and fighting officers had been hard to find with us. I said no more but told Grogan of the incident, telling him to watch this CO carefully. I don't think he was the man to command a battalion of young regular soldiers." (11)

What are we to make of this? On one level it was just Jack's enthusiasm for the coming fight that exuded from him. He was merely supporting and endorsing Ironside's words openly as he addressed the troops. To another commander it would have meant nothing more than the exuberance of exactly the sort of fighting man he needed - but to Ironside it was effrontery to speak when he was speaking. It is interesting that Ironside even mentions this minor episode until one realises the clashes between them that were to follow and that this part of his diary lays out already some sense of Jack being unbalanced and unfit for command. Interesting too that Ironside felt Jack unfit to command a roughly thrown together battalion of men when he had already successfully commanded experienced front line battalions in both Gallipoli and on the Somme - both facts again skilfully omitted from his description of Jack, as was the fact that Jack was a VC hero with a DSO as well. On another level then Ironside felt challenged by this larger than life heroic but colonial figure, confident and brusque, heady with the command of another battalion and another war to be fought. If Ironside was not up to the task of working with him then he would have to work without him - his warning to Grogan being a signal that any occasion to remove Kelly from command should be used. Within days then Jack was a marked man as far as Ironside was concerned.

Kelly and the Hampshires were loaded onto barges ready to be sent up the wide and flat River Dwina to Bereznik. Wearing the white star on a black background cloth insignia patch of the Relief Force, Kelly quickly started to make some maverick decisions. The risk of coming under fire as they slowly took the battalion up these open and undefended rivers was very real. Thus Kelly ordered the Hampshires to put all their Lewis and mounted machine guns on each side of the flat bottomed barges. Point outwards, these barges thus became modern day men o' war able to machine gun out of existence anyone opening fire on them. Quite remarkably the Regimental Museum of The Hampshire Regiment contains a photograph album of pictures of what are referred to as "Kelly's Mystery Ships". In another Jack can be seen standing tall, and a little thinner already, amongst his men in the heat, flies and mosquitoes of a north Russian mud flat. It was unorthodox and not in the army manual but undoubtedly effective. Jack Kelly was already aware that his men were outnumbered, outgunned and could easily be outflanked as they pressed on into the interior of Russia not sure if they were protecting the stores, bringing back the men already out there or being asked to destroy Bolshevism on the quiet.

By June 5th, Kelly was taking his men off the barges and taking over command of an area from the 339th United States Infantry who were pulling out. The United States populace were completely unaware that their men were even out there. However this theatre of war now became a solely British affair. By the 12th June Kelly was back into doing what he knew best. Although he had plenty of junior officers who should have been doing the patrolling of the area to work out what lay in front and to the side of them (there was after all no front line as in France), Kelly set the tone himself and led patrols deep into the woods around them. He was doing what his men already knew, showing he feared nothing and couldn't wait to get to grips with fighting this new enemy. This is what he loved and where he wanted to be - a long way from married life, from London and from Cranley Gardens. Having a Colonel of all things leading patrols from the front was most unusual and unorthodox but this was the man. The next day the Hampshires diary records:

'The C.O. took out No. One platoon of W Company and ran into a Bolo patrol in a neutral village. Two of the enemy were killed and one wounded. The C.O. killed one man in personal conflict.'

Not content with killing his first Bolshevik, Jack Kelly then took out another patrol on the 16th June:

"The C.O. took out 9 platoon on an all day reconnaissance of the route to Troitskoye. Marched 35 miles in 17 hours."

This was a huge patrol and would have exhausted even the fittest troops. Kelly was trying to obtain all the information he could of the surrounding geography especially the area around Troitskoye towards which the battalion would be moving if ordered further forward. Indeed his aggressive soldiering had already been praised with Brig Gen. Grogan writing to Kelly:

'The GOC wishes personally to thank you on the very gallant way you led the patrol on June 13th, 1919 which resulted in you killing three of the enemy at great personal risk to yourself. The information obtained by you was very valuable and the result of your encounter cannot but increase the morale of our men.'

What was dawning on Jack however was the vastness of the country and the minuscule size of the British forces now deep inside Russian territory. They were not large enough to either help the White Russians in any meaningful way to win the war against a Bolshevik enemy that had really already won their revolution. Equally they were not numerous enough to take on the Bolsheviks - poorly equipped and unreliable as they were - 8,000 men was not enough to enter and conquer Moscow for Churchill. Thus while Ironside still made plans for aggressive local actions and continued to plan actions in support of the local White Russian forces (all completely at odds with the avowed policy of Lloyd George and the government), Jack could see that there was no plan either to withdraw or invade and that the whole thing seemed pointless with men being sacrificed in the hope that the White Russians would somehow win victory and British forces would be there to support it - and of course protect and exploit the raw materials so heavily invested in by British business. This uncertainty must have played hard with Jack as he was ordered to prepare an attack on Troitskoye.

Partly to boost flagging Russian morale and partly attempting to link up with Russian forces further to the east, Ironside endorsed a plan for the 19th/20th June whereby the 3rd Russian rifles would launch an attack on the villages of Topsa and Troitskoye while Sherwood Kelly took two companies of the Hampshires on a nine mile trek through the stifling heat, horse flies and forests to appear behind the Bolshevik forces at the same time. During the development of the attack that morning Jack Kelly made one of the most important decisions of his life, although at the time he did not know it, in that he withdrew his men after waiting for six hours near their objective and just before the supporting Russian attack went in. As a result, although the Russians were jubilant, Ironside decided that Kelly had disobeyed orders and let down his Russian allies. The Hampshires Diary records that:

"Attacked at 04.45. At 10.30 as no news was heard or seen of 3rd N.R. Rifles on our right who were attacking Topsa and the enemy who were fighting very well nearly surrounded us, the C.O. decided to withdraw from the position we had reached round Troitskye village. After having withdrawn about two miles news was heard that

the 3rd N.R.Rifles had taken their objectives and Topsa so we marched into Topsa via the woods to the south."

If we have learnt anything about Jack it was that he was not afraid of a fight, indeed if he could create one he would - just to be able to take part. His actions at Troitskye were less to do with being frightened or 'having lost his head' as Ironside was to claim later, but more to do with practical considerations on the ground and his coming to the conclusion that further maximum effort to support the Russians was pointless. High handed maybe, certainly for the British Army, but in keeping with a man unafraid of making decisions. It was also possible that his VC gave him a heightened sense of his own importance elevating him in his own mind to a command level that he did not and would never have. He had after all been mixing with Generals on the boat over and, after being in the backwoods during 1918, he was now back in command of a battalion and with a VC on his chest too.

In his preparations for the attack, Kelly dragged his fit and experienced battalion on the march between 00.30 am and 04.00 am along tracks, through streams and across marshes which he knew well (he had after all already walked thirty five miles around it recently, further straining his gas damaged lungs). The regimental diary of the Hampshires confirms that the route up to Troitskye was awful and that the battalion had to cross two large marshes with swarms of mosquitos first unpacking their 60 mules and then manhandling their heavy equipment before going back to get the mules - at any moment they could have been ambushed and surrounded.

Arriving at their forming up position the battalion started to come under fire from the Bolsheviks at 04.45. They had learnt that Troitskye, far from being held by a small force of Bolsheviks, had in fact been reinforced in order to try to trap the British force which they also knew was coming towards them. The fire coming at the battalion was greater than one would have expected from a small unit so they were already exposed with a very difficult route out if they became surrounded and with absolutely no support behind them. He also found and complained later that communication lines with Brigade did not work. Kelly ordered Y company to emerge from the woods at 04.45 under cover of mortars and the machine guns that they had lugged up the tracks and through the marshes. After a few hours exchanging fire Kelly could see nothing of the expected White Russian advance nearby and had fifteen casualties including the young Capt. D.T.Gorman MC (buried at Archangel) who had been wounded five times serving in France, and Sergeant Batten who had seventeen years regular service and was now killed one hundred and eighteen miles inland from Archangel in the marshes of Northern Russia. Indeed it must have been heartbreaking for Jack to see Capt. Gorman, shot in the stomach, dragged for hours through 'that awful forest' only to die in agony sixteen hours later in Topsa. After six hours he then received reports that Bolshevik patrols were working their way around his rear. This together with no news of the Russian attack on Topsa made Kelly curse the local White Russians who had failed to turn up and indeed his own senior officers who had sent them there and decided to extract the battalion while he still could rather than risk being completely cut off and surrounded as the Regimental diary recorded:

"It was obvious that if the Russians failed (the attack at Topsa) our position would be most precarious, as if a withdrawl were

necessitated, we should have to march 18 miles through enemy country. Added to this was the fact that if we sustained heavy casualties we should not be able to evacuate them. The uncertainty of the situation undoubtedly weighed heavily on the CO especially as we were encountering more opposition than we had been led to expect. In addition the Bolos were working round our flanks in the most alarming manner and our position was becoming somewhat critical." (13)

So just a few days before The Treaty of Versailles was about to be signed in France on 28th June ending The Great War, the war in Russia was in full flow. The news of the Hampshires withdrawal seems to have been understood by Grogan without difficulty as the result of a sound decision by the CO on the ground, but it did not sit at all easily with Ironside who was subjected to a series of complaints sent through to him of Kelly's open criticism of his leadership. The final straw came when in late July Kelly was ordered to carry out a raid on Bolshevik blockhouses (bunkers defended by machine guns) under cover of gas. He quickly wrote a letter to Brigadier General Turner, the GOC of this area of the front, bypassing Grogan, saying that the attack would serve no purpose and his men would needlessly be killed in trying to impress the local but unreliable White Russian forces. However his tone was apparently high handed *"if the proposed operation is left to my discretion I shall not carry it out. I am continuing to make all preparations in case you order me to carry out the raid."*

Little by little Kelly was single handedly opposing the high command in Russia and Ironside would have no more second guessing of his orders, Jack was a marked man it would seem. Jack had already seen at first hand however that he and his men were being used and had decided that the campaign in Russia was a pointless waste of men and resources. While he had the best interests of his men at heart, he was in danger of crossing the line in a manner which the British Army could never tolerate. Indeed at his later Court Martial, although none of his senior officers in the battalion complained about Kelly's decisions and attitudes there was a statement from Lieutenant G.E.Hill, an Intelligence Officer, that stated that on the route back from Troitskye Kelly was openly complaining about the senior commanders in northern Russia and the Russians themselves:

Archangel
17th September 1919.

Sir,

I have the honour to report that on the night of the 19th/20th June 1919 in the capacity of Intelligence Officer, I accompanied the Column commanded by Lieut. Colonel Sherwood Kelly V.C., from KURGOMEN round the enemy flank to TROITSA with the object of capturing the latter.

During the march I was with Lieut. Colonel Sherwood Kelly at the head of the column and heard him continuously making remarks in a loud voice about the command in North Russia such as the following: "You cannot expect the show we are going on to succeed when we are commanded by a lot of people with no service like all these people out here. We will have to go through with this show, but it is no damn good. It is all very well for those damn people who sit on the ruddy backsides behind and run the show to tell us the Russians are going to fight, but I know they are not and we shall have to do the whole thing."

Later in the day, when the Column was resting after the operation, I heard Lieut. Colonel Sherwood Kelly say to his men:- "It is the Brigadier's fault that this show has failed but what can you expect, the man is only a very junior Major" or words to that effect. Owing to the length of time that has elapsed since events took place, I cannot repeat Lieut. Colonel Sherwood Kelly's words verbatim, but I can definitely state that both before and after the operation, Lieut. Colonel Sherwood Kelly's remarks to his men ridiculing his superiors, and especially Brigadier General Graham, were almost continuous and drew forth laughter from the men in the ranks.

> *I have the honour to be,*
> *Sir,*
> *Your obedient servant (14)*

Although Ironside was not aware of the specifics he was increasingly informed of Jack's open criticism. For Ironside the issue was not how to discipline Kelly but how to dress this matter up in a way that flagged up Kelly as the main reason for failure and not either Churchill's vacillation and duplicity, his own indecision and performance as a Commander, the hopelessness of the strategic situation or the massive problems of trying to work with loyal but disrupted White Russian units. Thus Ironside painted a picture of a man totally inept and who panicked, as he recorded in his diary:

"The Russian attack (on Troitskye) was a complete success. Over 500 prisoners taken and 100 dead were counted on the position. Unfortunately The Hampshires failed to take any part in the fight. Had they obeyed orders the result would have been an overwhelming success. The story was this. They duly arrived at their appointed

position some minutes before the zero hour, after a march of nine miles through the forest. They laid a cable behind them as they went and were all the time in communication with brigade headquarters. Just before the attack commenced some twenty or thirty of the enemy were seen coming up from their rear towards their front, apparently quite unaware of enemy troops being behind their line. The C.O. considered that he was being outflanked and withdrew his men some distance along the path by which he had come. He neither engaged the enemy party which he thought was outflanking him nor informed the brigade of what he was doing. Later he withdrew to his starting point without making any attempt to join in the fight which had then started.

When I interviewed the C.O. the next day he could not explain why he had acted as he had. He had obviously lost his head, thinking he had overshot his position and gone too far forward. It was a clear case of disobedience of orders, aggravated by the fact that he could have communicated with his superior at any moment. The effect of the non-cooperation of the British troops had a grave effect upon the Russians just at the very moment when they needed an overwhelming success to raise their morale. Had the CO been a regular officer I should certainly have had him court martialled. He had fought brilliantly throughout the war and now appeared to me to be worn out with the responsibility of having had to act in an isolated position. To put an end to the unfortunate incident I withdrew the battalion from the line, sending the CO down to base with orders that he should be sent home for demobilization."

Interpretation of events is the key role of the historian not judgment - this is for others to decide. When we assess what Ironside said in his account one could make the following interpretations:

Firstly, that Ironside included this event at all in his account was a deliberate attempt to put his side of the story and blacken the name of Kelly after his subsequent but not consequent court martial.

Secondly, it is clear that Ironside had already marked Kelly as insubordinate from the moment they met and a clash could only have been avoided if Jack ignored every passion and independent thought in his body. Jack had become more intemperate than ever and had the confidence of a man who had commanded two crack regular battalions in the war. The past three years had also seen Jack arrive in Britain with nothing and then proceed rapidly to hold the DSO, a CMG and VC, no doubt inflating his already heady self belief even further.

Thirdly, to say that Jack was worn out with responsibility of leading in an exposed position ignores the fact that he had been in this pointless position before at Cambrai and elsewhere, where after terrible sacrifice by his men, they waited for relief and support for two days before being asked to withdraw. He had no wish to repeat that experience with the lives of his men in North Russia, of all places, where there was absolutely no chance of support. He was not worn out with responsibility at all, he was simply unwilling to order brave men to die as a morale building exercise for unreliable Russian units and no doubt then be told to withdraw again. Ironside ignored the detail of the operational aspects whereas Jack Kelly on the ground, surrounded by unreliable Russian units, could sense that they were wasting lives.

Fourthly, anyone who knew Jack Kelly would know that he was one of the last persons on the planet with whom to have a face to face meeting. The probability is that there was a huge row between the 6'

4" mountain of man that was Kelly and the far more politically aware Ironside where Jack told him exactly what he thought of both the campaign itself as he could now see it and the conduct of operations. Jack was happy to kill Bolsheviks but not in some weak half hearted way or in a demonstration for morale boosting purposes. Where were the orders for a full assault, where were the men needed to do the job properly? Why was this whole thing being done on a shoe string with no-one in Britain aware that a war was being fought - "a shameful, illegitimate, little war?"

Fifthly, if Ironside had indeed threatened him with a court martial had he been a regular officer, this would have touched a raw nerve. Kelly would have demanded a Court Martial and no doubt dared Ironside to do it when Ironside pulled back from making this whole affair public, Jack Kelly made it happen anyway. Deep down there would have been a resentment that he was regarded as a colonial and had never been treated like a regular officer and that if a regular officer would have been court martialled then so should he. The kamikaze side of Jack's personality surfaced easily again.

Sixthly, rather like many a public school Headmaster of any age, Ironside had decided early on that Kelly was trouble and a bad hat and was having none of it. The high handed and arrogant way in which he ignored the facts surrounding the attack on Triotskye was breathtaking but typical of a man who had already decided the fate of the individual in front of him. With the war over there was no longer a need to tolerate such obstinacy or openness. Ironside's account was not only at odds with Kelly's version but also totally contradictory with the Regimental History - often very unbiased accounts put together from a range of sources.

Finally, Ironside may have wished to try to paint Kelly as a man who had lost his head and was out of his depth - but he had picked the wrong target. Ironside was not only wrong in his account of the action but also if he had thought Kelly was ever "worn out" as he put it he had another thing coming. All he had done was inflame the rage of an outrageous temper and provided Kelly with yet another battle.

There is also a considerable amount of other primary evidence to suggest that Kelly had done nothing wrong except challenge Ironside's authority. The Archangel war Diary for 20th June stated *"Enemy morale by no means low and were forewarned of attack by deserter from 4th North Russian Rifles."* In his excellent study of this whole episode Clifford Kinvig also cites an extract from a letter from one of Kelly's subalterns, a young lieutenant and VC winner himself who said *"...they gave us a very warm time but our own better shooting told heavily. However we were nearly surrounded and cut off so, fagged out as we were - we had to retreat at 9.30 am in the blazing heat, no rest, little food. My platoon was the last to leave, the enemy had worked up to within seventy yards, covering us with very heavy fire the whole time. We just got out and had to trek right back over our old trail, and we got back to TOPSA at 12 midnight."* (15) Kinvig also relates the comment of one Hampshires Sergeant who said of Col. Kelly *"He said he is not going to get any more of his men or officers killed for the sake of this ******country."*

Finally in Jack's complete defence we hear from Major Allfrey, of the companion Brigade, with his opinion of the Hampshires attack:

"In my opinion, and also Col. Davies's the show is tactically wrong...After five years of war good troops ought never to be placed in such a rotten predicament by some damn fool of a muddle headed

broken-down old regular soldier" - this being a reference to Brigadier General Graham who had planned the attack on Troitsa and Topsa."

Late Victorian and Edwardian social mores and standards had given Jack many a stage to play out his skirmishes and hostilities with authority figures but this was different. Ironside and Kelly were clearly on a serious collision course. As was his way, Jack decided to take on this challenge. On 26th July, the same day he took over command of the important Railway Front at Obozerskaya from White Russian Colonel Akutin, he wrote a letter to Mr E.E. Janson of Eaton Square in London criticizing the management and direction of the campaign in Russia and stating that the British soldiers who had volunteered were not actually pulling out at all but fighting 400 miles inland supporting local White Russian forces in the war against the Bolsheviks - explosive stuff given the attitude of much of the British public, the Trades Unions and the press:

> *2nd Hampshire Regiment*
> *26th July 1919*

My Dear Jan /

The position out here is, from a military point of view very critical - If the papers would publish the true state of affairs and cease advertising Ironside, who is weak and not fit for the job, (we have lost all confidence in him) it would be a good thing - He - ironside, has posed as the saviour of North Russia and will stick at nothing to save his face now that things have turned out contrary to expectation - For instance one reads such trash as "Ironsides Confidence Justified". Well the Russian Battalion to which that referred (Dyer's Btn) mutinied, murdered 12 officers 6 of whom were British and two companies joined the Bolo's - along with the M.G.C. of the 4th North R.Rifles - Another advert is - "A Hercules in Khaki and builder of an Anti-Bolshevik Army" - well the whole of the Onega front 4,000 Russians trained and armed and clothed by Ironside have all gone over to the Bolo's killing or capturing all British Officers with them - We are here, on railway front, sent from Pinega, to quell mutiny of Russian troops - You can make what use you like of this letter and it is your duty in the interests of the British here to expose the show.

Love to you both - Jonnie.

OAS
E.W.Janson Esq
11 Eaton Mansions
Eton Square, London (16)

Jack knew full well that his letters may not get through the army censor so just to be certain one got through (or indeed hit the censor's eye) he added the following to his second letter to Mrs Cameron on the same day:

The position out here at present is <u>very serious</u> - it is time things were correctly reported in the papers - Since last I wrote we have been moved from the Pinega front to the Valogda Railway front - some 200 miles from Pinega - The whole of the Russians on the Onega front 4,000 in all have joined the Bolsheviks murdering or capturing <u>all</u> the British Officers with them - The Russian troops <u>everywhere</u> are turning against us - So much for Ironside's Anti-Bolshevik Army - The whole show is one huge advert for him - It is time some strong reliable man was sent out - We have lost all confidence in Ironside and are sick of reading the lying statements of what he is supposed to be doing.

Neither letter made it through the censors. Instead in early August they were opened by the censor in England who immediately realized what he had in his hands. Jack later claimed that he had written the letters knowing that they would be opened and that this would give him an opportunity to tell the public of this *"useless, aimless and ill managed campaign"* and that he was *"determined to get back by some means or other to England."* Within days Ironside had been informed and was in a rage. Brigadier Turner was asked for a report on Kelly. He stated openly that *"He is a hot headed and quarrelsome man who has rows with practically everyone with whom he has come into contact."* Turner however went on to say *"He has a fine smart well-drilled battalion and his men like him but I do not consider he is suitable for command of a regular battalion under the present conditions"* - in other words he was a good soldier, strong leader of men, well liked and courageous but he did not toe the line, and spoke his mind. The current conflict, with its political overtones, could not depend on his support and he could not be prevented from speaking out against the orders being given. In truth Turner was right in that men like Jack had been a necessity during the war but in peacetime he would have been very unlikely to have either risen so high in rank that he had or commanded a regular battalion.

This explosive situation smouldered on throughout July and early August and caused problems for the officers around him. Grogan seems to have been understanding of Kelly's actions at Troitskya but saw Jack's single handed challenge to the authority of GHQ staff as irritating. At one point Jack had told Grogan over the telephone that the whole affair was a shambles and that if he was a party to all this he needed his head tested! Later at his subsequent court martial Jack even admitted that:

'I did in fact make myself thoroughly unpopular at GHQ. So much so that General Grogan said to me that it would be a source of the greatest satisfaction on the part of General Ironsides staff if I was sent home. However on every occasion I have come into contact with the staff my motives have been a very real concern for the well being of the officers and men.'

Jack thought that he had an implicit agreement with Ironside not to take the matter further with General Sir Henry Rawlinson who was now the Commander in Chief in north Russia. During August the Hampshires had little to do but Jack continued in command with his junior officers well aware of what had happened. However Ironside either did not make such an undertaking with Kelly or went back on his word and wrote to Rawlinson pointing out that he thought Kelly had lost his head, had not recovered from his wounds received in 1916 and should be sent home in disgrace. On 15st August Jack was sitting at his desk in his command tent when his signal officer brought in a message from Ironside stating that he had discussed the matter with General Rawlinson and it had been agreed that Jack was to be removed from his command on the 18th August and sent home as recorded by Brigadier General Turner:

On the 18th August, under instructions from GHQ, Colonel Kelly was relieved of his Command.

Except for the above mentioned incident (where Jack had made changes to front line dispositions without consulting Turner) during the time Colonel Kelly has been with me no difficulty or question has arisen between us ; our relations have been most cordial, and to the best of my belief he has loyally supported me in every way, and as Colonel Kelly was thoroughly conversant with my plans for withdrawal, I deprecated his removal so soon before it was likely the plans might have to be set in force.

The battalion under his command was in a thoroughly efficient state and well disciplined....

Jack was enraged beyond control. The whole Russian affair was enough to make his blood boil and in its waste of time and men but the explosive point was the attack on his honour and character which he was not prepared to allow to happen. Jack now chose to expose the whole affair to the British people partly to warn them about what was going on - a war on Bolshevism not a withdrawal - but also to expose those in command over him who had ganged together to destroy his reputation. Maybe his temper now got the better of him. This was to be a personal war between Jack and the whole British Establishment. He packed his bags and said his goodbyes both to his officers in the battalion and his men - he had not been relieved of command ever before in his life and the level of injustice he felt was unbearable to such a proud man. Walking out and off the jetty to his boat home, he resolved that he was not going to let Ironside, Rawlinson, Grogan and especially Churchill get away with what he saw as the gross manipulation of both the British public and the men who had volunteered to go to Russia.

On board his six day journey home he wrote a letter to The Daily Express, the newspaper that had been so keen to watch Churchill's plans in north Russia, stating:

'I ask you, Sir, to publish this letter so that people in England may know the truth about the situation in Archangel and may be able to take steps to right it.'

On Saturday 6th September 1919, Lt. Colonel Jack Sherwood Kelly suddenly became a household name as his letter and photograph were splashed across the front pages of The Daily Express. If it was notoriety he wanted he had it, if it was justice he craved he was to be disappointed.

Archangel Scandal Exposed

Duplicity of Churchill Policy in Russia

The Public Humbugged

Famous VC appeals to the Nation

Such were the headlines that greeted Churchill, the Cabinet, Lloyd George and the officers of the General Staff that weekend. Kelly had done a good job. It was a cutting, no holds barred attack on both British policy in North Russia and the way in which operations were being carried out as such he was attacking and criticising both Churchill and Ironside. He said he had volunteered for the Relief Force in the sincere belief that relief was urgently needed in order to make possible the withdrawal of low category troops in the last stage of exhaustion due to fierce fighting among the rigours of an Arctic winter. But he went on:

"I was reluctantly but inevitably drawn to the following conclusion: That the troops of the Relief Force which we were told had been sent out for purely defensive purposes, were being used for offensive purposes on a large scale and far into the interior, in furtherance of some ambitious plan of campaign the nature of which we were not allowed to know. My personal experience of those operations was

that they were not even well conducted and they were not calculated to benefit in a military or any other sense a sound and practical British policy in Russia. They only entailed useless loss and suffering in troops that had already made great sacrifices in the Great War."

Not content with those broadsides, Jack vented his spleen on the *"much vaunted 'loyal Russian Army', composed largely of Bolshevik prisoners dressed khaki"* and the *"puppet government set up by us in Archangel..."*

The reaction of the British press and the Trades Union movement was electric. Here at last was clear evidence placed before everyone of what they had feared and Churchill's plans to at least wait and see what would happen in Russia and at most to use the Relief Force to actively fight alongside the White Russians was exposed. Immediately there was dramatic reaction and activity in the House of Commons. Jack meanwhile, had arrived back in London and unpacked probably at the Rubens Hotel near Victoria which was to be his home for the next few months. We do not know how Nellie was reacting to all this but just to have him home was probably enough and with this new conflict to fight, he was at least in good spirits! With the game exposed so effectively, Churchill began to prepare his ground to survive the storm. Lloyd George could see that such a scandal could do enormous damage and that Kelly had unleashed a demon from the bottle that could engulf the whole government. The next few days saw constant reports, anger and criticism throughout the press. Pressure increased on both the government, Churchill and The War Office. Standing where he liked to be, alone, Jack received a letter from The War Office on September 13th coinciding with a statement from Winston Churchill in The House of Commons the previous evening. Clearly Churchill had held several meetings to plan the best way out of this mess and decided to use eloquence and military justice rather than answer Jack's charges in any detail. Of course Jack did not realize what he was up against now. He was used to face to face combat either with words or bullets but Churchill's weapons of subtle insinuation were used at distance and with the authority of one who knew how to escape from almost any situation. The key section of Churchill's statement read:

"To add to the difficulties of such an operation in its most critical phase, by inspiring the enemy, or disarming the Russian national Forces or by spreading despondency among our troops, is wrong and unpatriotic. In a military officer such conduct is a grave offence. In this connection attention must be drawn particularly to the statements which have been published purporting to emanate from Lt. Colonel Sherwood Kelly."

Suddenly, deftly and without effort, Churchill had evaded Jack's initial challenge on the matter of what was happening in Russia itself and turned the matter into questioning Kelly's character, patriotism and role in undermining the morale of British troops in North Russia. The goalposts were moving fast and Jack could now sense that he was in a game where the rules were made by others. The statement continued:

'This officer was, on 16th August, removed from his command at Archangel and sent back to England by General Rawlinson for a serious offence under the Army Act. General Rawlinson has reported that he refrained from trial by court martial only on account of his gallant fighting record.'

Again, the words were chosen carefully to imply that Rawlinson had been sensitive to Kelly who clearly had been guilty of some grave but unspecified offence. To the general reader and to Jack this could have meant anything, cowardice and inciting the troops to mutiny or treason being the most obvious. The statement concluded:

'He has now been alleged to have committed an offence of a different character against King's regulations in regard to which disciplinary action must take its course.'

Jack was out of his depth and drowning rapidly. His violent temper coupled with his deep rooted problems with authority had become confused with a genuine frustration at the waste of British lives in a futile campaign in Russia in which he felt he and his men had been duped into volunteering. But the issue was now about challenging and taking on the government to protect his honour and this, as is so often the case, saw discretion fly out of the window in favour of valour. Like a drowning man he clutched at every straw and the day before the War Office statement was published, Jack sent a letter to Mr. Thomas M.P. who was due to speak at The Trades Union Congress in Glasgow on 13th September about the whole scandalous Russian affair. On the same morning that he received his letter from The War Office Jack wrote a second letter to The Daily Express. Why did he do this? Undoutedly, because he knew he needed support. The Army would not help him, his colleagues had he felt deserted him and the Conservative and Liberal Parties would disavow him. Though far from being a socialist, Jack knew that their voice would be a loud one in his favour. On September 13th The Times and The Daily Express carried both Jack's second letter and a report on Mr. Thomas's speech at The TUC:

COL. SHERWOOD KELLY'S REPLY TO
MR. CHURCHILL'S CHARGES

WHAT HIS "SERIOUS OFFENCE" WAS

The only way of calling public attention to the Russian Scandal

DEMAND FOR A COURT MARTIAL

In this second and longer letter splashed across the front pages of the national press, Jack Sherwood Kelly took a giant stride further than ever before, naming all the senior military officers who had been involved in the arguments and obvious deceptions in Russia. Jack stated that he had not intended to rush into print but he had been given no alternative. Now it was his personal honour that was at stake. He stated that Churchill's wording was deliberately distorted (in this he was of course correct) and could have meant anything. The letter carried a series of explanations of his conduct which he claimed to have always been founded on protecting his men in what he saw as a pointless strategy where they were being used and killed for a plan initiated by Churchill against the wishes and knowledge of the British people. Jack published letters he had received from Grogan and his letters of concern to Turner. Jack then explained what the so called "Serious Offence" was (which were letters homed to his friends) not cowardice as Churchill and the War Office were trying to imply. Jack also went on to produce a telegram from Turner sent to Rawlinson just before he met with Jack on the 16th August.

15.8.19 Presume this officer (Kelly) is only required temporarily at Archangel. I do not wish to lose his services at this juncture. Things are now working quite smoothly.

This was the same Turner who had previously commented on Jack that he was not suited to the command of a battalion at this time - could it be that Jack was just difficult and hot headed until one knew how to take him? Clearly Turner did not consider Jack deserved to be relieved of command even if Ironside had made up his mind that he would be. The rest of the letter then dealt with the duplicity with which Jack felt he had been treated by both Rawlinson and Ironside saying what they needed to his face just to get him on a boat home and then dropping him from command and any promises that they might have made to give him a new battalion in England. Finally, Jack stated that they had threatened him with a court martial and that he hoped that this second letter would provide one so that he could clear his name.

To Thomas at the TUC, Kelly's actions were far more glorious. He sensed that Churchill's timing had been excellent - issuing his denials the day before the Congress began and passing the matters from his own hands and his own responsibility back to the Army for their justice to run its course. Mr Thomas, referring to Jack as "the gallant Colonel Kelly," went on to say that Jack knew exactly what he was giving up when he wrote his letters - his career and his future but that he had not expected to give up his honour too. Mr Thomas hoped that the court martial would be in public and that the government would answer the charges against them of duplicity. He also hoped that parliament would hold its own court martial on Churchill and ensure that the facts were made known to the British public.

The Daily Express spent the rest of September attacking Churchill and his "private war" and Churchill must have felt real venom towards Jack Kelly that month - this could have finished Churchill's career. Outbursts of support for Kelly and anger against the government were recorded in Liverpool, Newcastle, Nottingham and Glasgow. On October 6th Jack wrote yet a third letter to the Daily Express commenting on the news that British troops had all been withdrawn from Archangel. He stated that it was the exposure of Churchill's policy that had speeded up the decision to pull out completely - and he was probably right. Churchill faced numerous questions in the house, notably on 22nd October where a certain MP Mr Thomas was also keen to know what was still going on in Russia and about how much the whole episode had cost? Churchill skilfully avoided identifying this figure, and whether British warships and troops were still engaged in operations in North Russia. At the same time as Churchill was fuming at being trumped and was being forced into unpicking his plan, Jack once again became something of a celebrity and relations with Nellie improved as she and he dodged reporters on their Kensington doorstep. Finally, Jack was ordered to present himself before a Court Martial held at Middlesex Guildhall on October 28th. The irony of Churchill sitting in the House of Commons while across Parliament Square Jack Kelly was being Court Martialled is deep.

He was not in the mood to compromise. He had done what he had done not because he was opposed to an all out war against the Bolsheviks but because of the half hearted and under handed way in which it had been done and at the needless waste of men's lives. He also had felt that the matter had spiralled from an issue over Russia into accusations about his personal conduct and honour and this demanded redress. He of course continued to drag Ironside, Rawlinson and Grogan into the enquiry clearly feeling that their reputations needed bruising as much as his own. They of course kept silent on the whole matter throughout. Predictably the Army closed ranks and had to disavow what Jack had done but equally predictably they did not want to make Jack a martyr. He had after all a superb fighting record. And what he had said about Churchill's Russian policy was true and what was desired was to brush him under the carpet as quickly and as quietly as possible. Jack's own defence ended with his stating:

"What is my responsibility? I was a volunteer and went to Russia because I was led to believe that the small British force that spent the winter there was in great peril. We were told that this was a defensive measure and that we were being sent to rescue the lives of our comrades whose position was hopeless.

I went determined to do my best. Ninety percent of my battalion consisted of officers and men who had served their King and Country throughout the great war and I felt they had the right to live and that their lives were too valuable to sacrifice , besides the money that was being squandered and the politicians responsible for the waste of those British lives in the Russian scandal should be brought to trial.

I have carried out my duty to the best of my skill and ability. Loyalty to the Throne is with me a paramount ideal. I have sacrificed everything to carry those ideals into action. I have nothing left but a soldier's honour so I plead with you to believe that the action I took was to protect my men's lives against needless sacrifice and to save the country from squandering wealth she could ill afford. I leave this matter in your hands hoping you will remember my past services to my King and Country."

Jack watched as the court martial acted fast in hearing the accusations and defence and then handing down its sentence - a severe reprimand - the lightest that a court martial could confer.

Churchill of course was nowhere and everywhere. Did Jack feel vindicated? We do not know. We do know that Nellie was with him in court as were many reporters - but not as many as were covering the sports events of the time. Did he affect the careers of those officers who had impugned his honour? Well surprisingly enough perhaps he did. On his return home from Russia, Ironside, far from having his Major General's rank confirmed and being treated like a hero for holding the fort and bringing back the men, was actually reverted in rank back to Colonel (subsequently Ironside's career took him to Inspector General of the Overseas Forces, a post that was dissolved from under him, and he was removed rapidly from his appointment as Chief of the Imperial General Staff which was also removed from him when the British Army collapsed in May 1940 (- maybe Jack sensed all along that although a good soldier he was not a battle field commander). At the same time he was put on half pay with no job to go to. Was this in any way the result of his mishandling Jack Sherwood Kelly and this whole sorry episode? We will never know but it is hardly the reaction of a grateful Secretary of War. Did Kelly affect the withdrawal from Russia - almost certainly? There would have been many meetings behind closed doors between Churchill and other members of the Cabinet with the Prime Minister probably telling him what a bloody headstrong fool he had been and that now he was up against yet an even bigger bloody headstrong fool determined to bring him down, but that was not going to be allowed to happen. The men were to be withdrawn from Russia immediately, as all hope of saving Russia from Bolshevism had gone and Kelly as a critic was to be neutralized. The hope was that Kelly would go quietly. He did but he was not finished fighting yet.

There are two footnotes to this whole episode. Lest we be in any doubt as to Churchill's hidden agenda, one is to be found in the pages of Punch magazine, or The London Charivari as it was then known. In the edition published August 20th 1919 on page 174 a small item appears at the bottom of the page:

"After 5 years the famous story of Russian soldiers training in England has come true. At this very moment, one thousand White Russian Army officers are receiving military training at Newmarket. The announcement greatly shocked Captain Wedgewood Benn who thought it a dreadful thing that Russian officers should be trained by us to fight against their own Government. But not so said Mr Churchill. The object was merely to enable them to relieve our own officers and men. The House as a whole was satisfied with this answer."

Secondly, the White Russian Awards given out after 1919 to all members of the Royal Air Force, Royal Navy and The Army did not include the name of Lt. Col. Jack Sherwood Kelly.

And so the show went on. The bodies of more than 600 British servicemen were buried in Northern Russia and the total cost of this latest Churchillian was calculated at a staggering £49,631,000. Churchill was as we know to continue his roller coaster career but so too, on a different stage, was Jack.

(1)   Regimental Journal of The Hampshire Regiment

(2)   Rose - King George V

(3)   Rhodes James - Churchill

(4)   The Daily Express

(5)   National Archives, Kew

(6)   'Churchill's Crusade: The British Invasion of Russia, 1918-1920'
        by Clifford Kinvig. (Continuum, 2006) ISBN 1852854772

(7)   Oscar Wilde from The Importance of Being Earnest

(8)   'The Day we Almost Bombed Moscow' by Christopher Dobson &
        John Miller. (Hodder & Stoughton) p.177

(9)   Quoted in 'Archangel 1918-1919' by Edmund Ironside.
        (Constable, London), p.117

(10)   Allfrey, 'Five Months', pp.1-2; Kettle, Archangel Fiasco, p.542

(11)   Ibid. p.145

(12)   Regimental Journal of The Hampshire Regiment

(13)   Imperial War Museum, 74/29/1, Letter of Lieutenant M.S.Moore,
        25th June, 1919

(14)   National Archives, Kew

(15)   Ibid. Kinvig

(16)   National Archives, Kew

CHAPTER EIGHT

'The current building was erected in 1911 to house debutantes from the Shires residing in London for their Coming Out Season ... as such the building was used as a hostel for young ladies visiting the Palace.'

- From The History of The Rubens Hotel.

A THIRD LIFE, 1919-1926

The Christmas of 1919 for Jack and Nellie was a strange one. Quite clearly the exertions of the previous few months both in Russia physically and in London mentally and emotionally had drained Jack. Beside him throughout these months of turmoil had been Nellie. Despite the ravages of his temper, the pressures of his infidelity, his letters to the press and his uncontrollable rage she still loved him. It took a few weeks of inactivity to show Jack that his world had changed for good. The world around him was one of peacetime and getting back into a normal routine of family life - something he knew nothing about. His whole world had been engulfed by war for nearly five continuous years and he had embraced it. Now he had to set off in the mornings dressing in civilian clothes as he was put on half pay alongside Ironside as The War Office decided how many men it needed and could afford in its peacetime army - and who they would be.

Between 1920 and 1922 Jack was adjusting to being with Nellie too. Often resident at the Hotel Rubens, Jack would have been invited to many events and parties. The Rubens had been opened in 1911 and was the most popular place in London for debutante parties during the war with the ballroom holding a major event almost every week.

The divorce had been postponed and we know that he wrote many times to the War Office trying, unsuccessfully, to get a military job. Either they had nothing for him or more likely he was now a permanent black sheep. We do know that Jack's hatred of Bolshevism was very real. He had seen what it meant at first hand and recognized, as Churchill had done, that it meant the end of liberty, freedom and the Empire - in fact all that he stood for. He had already said that he was happy to crush Bolshevism if the resources and will power were provided and in the summer of 1919 he was able to show first hand his willingness to sacrifice himself for what he believed.

Grumbling discontent amongst the police force had, by 1918, manifested itself in direct action. For the first time the government witnessed the potential power of the trades unions amongst their own organs of control over the people. In August 1918 a whole series of strikes called by the National Union of Police and Prison Officers (NUPPO) saw The Metropolitan Police go on strike. This had never happened before and the strike and union were in fact banned by the then Police Commissioner Sir Edward Henry. However this did not stop a strike from developing across London. The war was not yet over, the Labour party was only reliable for support as long as the war continued and union activity was spreading across the country - there were even plenty of Bolshevik agitators working away leaving fear and rumour in their wake. The demands of NUPPO were simple - a pay increase and better pension rights but also recognition of the union. The government panicked and gave into all demands except recognition of the Union - however NUPPO's membership swelled from the ten thousand Metropolitan officers to fifty thousand across the country. By the end of 1918 numerous unions were active and by the summer of 1919 there were strikes across Britain. As Jack stepped off ship the press was already saying that a Bolshevik revolution had arrived in Britain. As if his problems with Churchill, the British Army and government were not enough, Jack, in the midst of all his letter writing, was not to be found quietly seeking the advice of Nellie as to his future, not keeping a low profile in Cranley Gardens or The Hotel Rubens as events unfolded, but immediately fighting another little private war. The two main unions that struck in favour of the Police were the railway and transport workers. London was quickly coming to a standstill and Jack, along with other professionals from law firms, the army, navy, civil service and many sections of London society came out on the streets and volunteered to keep London working as the working man stood back and watched. It was a remarkable sight. Trams could be seen being pulled down London's streets not by horses but by men and buses were being driven by judges not bus drivers. London was displaying its characteristically robust reaction to being held to ransom. Jack himself volunteered to work as a stableman in the Southern Railway at Blackfriars. Understandably given that most of his youth was spent with horses, he was able to feed and muck them out as well as hitch them to wagons and trams. The company offered him pay but Jack declined to accept and instead asked that an equivalent sum be handed to The Waifs and Strays Society for homeless children.

Quite what happened next is unclear but evidently he had once again fallen out with Nellie. The next reference that we have is a newspaper report dated 20th November 1922. In it we discover that Jack found himself called to the Windsor Magistrates Court for non payment of his gas bill. Stating that he was both insolvent and in hospital awaiting an operation and could not work due to wounds received during the war must have made this the lowest point in Jack's life.

Marriage to Nellie had either ended in divorce, although there is no record of this, or permanent separation. She was a woman of substantial means and even Jack would not have been able to spend his way through her fortune. Also the fact that he was summoned by the Windsor Court suggest that he had moved away from London - perhaps to get away from the press where he did not want to be seen on hard times. We can also assume that his wounds and the exertions of 1919 had finally caught up with him. In any event the magistrate, in consideration of the Colonels' war service, adjourned the case for three months - which no doubt gave him time to find the money for the gas bill. But where was Nellie?

If we assume that for around two years between 1920 and 1922 Jack and Nellie were separated that would explain why in 1922 Jack's personal fortunes started to pick up again. Many men would no doubt have succumbed to the pressures of civilian life after all that he had gone through. On 25th November 1918 The Times carried a quotation from a speech delivered two days before by David Lloyd George. In it Lloyd George had promised that the land must become a 'home fit for heroes.' Fine election stuff but for Jack and millions of others who could testify to the fact, England was never to be that place. Suicide rates for returned soldiers were very high, almost fifteen times the rate before the war as men were unable to adjust to failed relationships, careers that no longer existed, a society that had changed behind their backs and an England where the codes of valour and service that they had fought for had been eroded. There was no special treatment for a man who woke up every night in a cold sweat because the noise of a car sounded like a shell about to fall on them. Post Traumatic Stress Disorder affected millions not just a few and Jack may have been in his own way too. Maybe however, just maybe he had started to mellow in his emotional needs. By the summer of 1922 Jack had in any event returned to a relationship of sorts with Nellie.

Whilst researching this book in 1991, a newspaper article in Norfolk was published in the wonderful Eastern Daily Press carrying some of the material that was then available about Jack's life. Out of the blue in one of those magical moments of history I received a telephone call from Mr. W.R.Morris a resident of Bungay in Suffolk. He told me that he had known Lt. Colonel Jack Sherwood Kelly in the early 1920s. To do justice to the then 86 year old Mr. Morris let us allow him to take us verbatim through his memories:

"I was born in 1905 and went to London to work in 1921 starting on the 29th September. My first job was as an office boy for a firm of solicitors at Number 4 Lincoln's Inn. The buildings were very grand near Chancery Lane and very old and ornate, I had never seen anything like them. I worked doing all sorts of jobs. I had to keep smart and clean and my collars were taken off every night to be washed and starched before I put them on the same shirt every day - I only had one shirt.

I worked for a Leonard Alfred Lauraine North - he was the only partner at the start but there were many more later. I was paid 12 shillings a week and my main job was to lick stamps and to run errands. In the late part of 1922 I started to see Lt. Colonel Kelly come into the offices. He would arrive through the door looking huge. He had a solid face and fixed smile and was a huge man - you couldn't see the light from outside behind him as he came in. He would crack his stick down on the table and say good morning and then started to take off his bowler hat and gloves. He never wore an overcoat no matter what the weather and you could tell he was a military man. He always had a blue or black pin striped suit, with a white collar and tie and very shiny shoes. He had a thin moustache and looked a very strong and confident man - you wouldn't want to argue with him. If we saw him coming through the window we would all jump to attention taking the micky before he opened the door - but we were very serious when he was in.

He would wait and then his wife would arrive - or sometimes they would arrive together and he would say 'Col. and Mrs. Sherwood Kelly to see Mr. North'. She was immaculately dressed and looked to us like a film star, a yahoo, a stunner. Very tall and thin but very gentle and quiet, they were very different. She had a ton of money.

Mrs. Sherwood Kelly would go in to Mr. North alone and the Colonel would pace around in the outer office. He sometimes talked to us but it was very brisk. Mr. North would write a letter to a firm of Stockbrokers called Forster and Braithwaite at 27 Austin Friars London EC2 and I would be given 2d to run the letter over by hand. Sometimes the letters contained instructions to buy £500 of ICI or Boots The Chemists shares and at other times they would be instructions to sell shares and I would bring back a bankers draft or even notes. This carried on during 1923 and clearly they were a partnership sometimes buying and sometimes selling but it was all her money.

We heard about him trying to become an MP in 1923 and read in the newspapers that he had beaten some chap up for being rude to him. That did not surprise us in the least. He was a strong talking man of few words, talked very English but we liked him. But by 1924 they stopped coming in together and he became very aggressive. He would march in, bang his stick down and bark out Sherwood Kelly for Mr. North! We had heard that he and Mrs. Sherwood Kelly had divorced because Mr. North had arranged part of a financial settlement for Col. Kelly. There was no fuss, I think it all went through very smoothly with no names in the press. He would go through and see Mr. North himself and all I would do is take letters to sell shares and the money went to Col. Kelly. I was always astonished at the amounts that he took each month - you could buy a very nice house for under £500 in those days. He stopped coming around 1925 but I never saw her again."

Clearly Jack and Nellie had come back together once more and for what would be the final period in their lives. Apart from the fact that she no doubt was his financial salvation, we can assume that they had at this time a high level of social status once more as a couple. Jack's health problems would always be there as his body had been so badly damaged by gas and bullets but even so the amounts of money being used or traded were considerable.

Apart from winning Nellie's affections back, one of the more incredible aspects of Jacks life was his determination to go into politics. What drove him to this conclusion given the way politicians had ruined his military career is an open question. It might have been because he saw that there were more battles to be fought but more likely it was because Nellie's brother William Pomeroy Crawford Greene, who had also survived the war, had announced he was going to stand for parliament at the next election in 1923 as a Conservative candidate. It was possible that William saw a chance to redirect and channel Jack's energy and drive into a political career and thus possibly save the marriage. In any event Jack put his name forward to the Conservative Party to stand as a parliamentary candidate and he was allocated the staunchly Socialist/ Labour party seat of Clay

Cross in Derbyshire. There was probably no harder seat to win in the country but Jack set about campaigning in this perfect example of a town and area created by the industrial revolution.

Alongside him on the trail was Nellie once more giving her best to the man she continued to love despite all that had transpired. The political scene was one of division and realignment. The war years had thrown everything into chaos in terms of political development but now there was a genuine three party structure with Labour stealing support from both the liberals and conservatives. In Clay Cross the potential for a Conservative candidate to take the seat was almost zero but in the election of 5th December 1923, Jack Kelly pushed the Liberals down into third place and received 4,881 votes - against the 11,939 of Mr. Charles Duncan MP. It was as though Jack was once again leading his troops into combat as the general election gave him another battle field on which to fight. It was during this series of meetings that Jack found Jack Johnson who had saved his life back in 1916 on The Somme. The Derbyshire Times reported that:

'...the result was declared between half past two and three o'clock but owing to a torrential downpour there were few people in the precincts of the schoolyard but the drill hall attached was packed with supporters of the Labour candidate. The presiding officer announced the figures there, the result being greeted with rounds of applause.

Lt. Col. Kelly remarked that he did not think any other constituency in England had been fought cleaner and better, and with less acrimony than at Clay Cross. From start to finish it had been a friendly contest and he congratulated 'Our Member' on his success.

Lt. Col. Kelly intimated that he would fight the seat again. He thanked all who had worked magnificently. "It has been a fine clean fight and I congratulate our MP."

However of equal interest and the only factual evidence of Nellie's thoughts the paper went on:

"Mrs Sherwood Kelly was also anxious to thank the electors. She said "We have made many staunch friends and we hope to come and live amongst you."

Undaunted Jack and Nellie Sherwood Kelly returned to London closer than ever before and motivated and energized by the challenges of speaking out for what Jack believed. Even the normally quiet and reserved Nellie played the part perfectly of the loyal and patriotic wife. Jack supported local political activists in London throughout 1924 and watched as the Conservative Party under Stanley Baldwin grew in popularity and the Liberals under Herbert Asquith watched as their party disintegrated around them. Both Nellie and Jack spent as much time as they could meeting and greeting local party supporters in and around Clay Cross and prepared the way for a second run at the seat. Before they could do that it was necessary to be adopted again by the local constituency party.

Col. Sherwood Kelly VC Adopted by The Conservatives

'There was a representative gathering at Clay Cross Drill Hall on Wednesday under the auspices of the Clay Cross Unionist Association. Dr. F. Marriott president of the Association occupied the chair and remarked that Col. Sherwood Kelly made such an

excellent impression from one end of the constituency to the other that the Executive of the Association felt that they could not do better than to invite him to come again. In his opinion Col. Kelly was the best man to represent the Clay Cross division in the House of Commons. They had to show the Socialists and Bolsheviks that they were up against Englishmen - Englishmen to whom no difficulty was too great to overcome.'

Jack had found a new battleground and a new side to himself - speechmaker and political leader. His experience the previous year had encouraged him to believe that he could win this seat and Nellie was there to back him. His enthusiasm always had been one of the key aspects of his inspirational leadership - and he was energised by the thought of entering parliament although Churchill may not have really looked forward to that particular prospect with great eagerness.

In one newspaper report headed 'The Red Flag or The Union Jack', Jack really gave a masterly performance and we can see just how far his eloquence had developed and justice to Jack's energy and fire can only be done by reading the full report.

'Col. Sherwood Kelly was enthusiastically received and at the outset said that they had to decide at this election whether they were to be governed by The Red Flag or The Union Jack. There were a good many English people who did not appreciate what the Union Jack meant abroad. Englishmen always woke up at a crisis and they had reached a crisis today - a crisis brought about by the Communists whom he called "Sluts!" Are we he asked to be governed by the British House of Commons or from Moscow! Mr. Stanley Baldwin and the Conservatives stood four square for God, King and Empire.

It was left to the Conservatives, as it always was, to retrieve a situation at a crisis. Well they had been awakened and their enemies would wish they had never roused them up! (Cheers and Applause). And now they were awakened all of them would have to put their whole hearts and souls into it to save the Empire. All sorts of promises were made at the last election, but what had been done for the men who won the war - our British Tommies - who are the British workmen, for it was from amongst them that the Tommies were drawn? Everyone knew what he thought of the British Tommy: he had proved it over and over again. The men who won the war saved England, and were going to save England again at this election. (Cheers) The working men realized that they had been gulled at the last election and they were determined not to be gulled again. They had no desire to be governed from Moscow. (Applause) Why should we make a loan to Russia to enable the Bolsheviks to carry on propaganda for the destruction of the British Empire? In Mister Stanley Baldwin we had a fine, sturdy Englishman - not a firebrand - who would save the Empire for us. "If I get in, and I'm going to get in this time...." (The remainder of the sentence was lost in the loud cheering). In thanking the audience for his wonderful reception, the Colonel said that if he was beaten this time he should come again, but there was no such thing as being beaten this time. (Cheers) The solid British working man would be behind the Conservatives in their stand against the menace of Bolshevism and Socialism (Applause). "

The motion to adopt Jack Kelly was carried unanimously and the hall erupted into a fever of noise, red faces, cheering and back slapping. Jack, reading and sensing the euphoric temperature of the meeting, concluded the evening by saying that if he were returned for the seat he hoped he would live up to what they expected of him and he hoped that they realized that if he said a thing he meant it, and nothing would turn him back from any pledge he made. The applause rang out loud and long and his supporters left thinking that far from Clay Cross being a lost cause to the Conservatives that with Lt. Col. Kelly leading the charge that they had at least a chance. For Jack and Nellie the whole experience was bringing them closer together than they had ever been before. At last they had a reason to work together and to be together and Nellie had never been happier. She could see Jack in his element and understand why his men thought so much of him. He was glad to shake hands as he walked the streets, his larger than life confidence blazed out of him drawing people nearer and exuding a magnetic wave of charisma and charm that, combined with his tremendous open confidence, turned heads and made people believe that here really was a politician that cared and who would deliver regardless of the cost.

Two days later Jack was out on the street addressing public meetings around the constituency, up against it but at his best. Clay Cross was already a strongly established hotbed of socialist fervour where Conservatives and Unionists and all that they stood for were resented and indeed hated. As the pace increased and polling day set for October 29th 1923 approached, the words used became more powerful and provocative and Jack's increasing popularity was certainly a worry for the local Labour party. On October 24th, with only five days to go, Jack and Nellie arrived at Langwith for an evening on the hustings in the school hall against the local Labour partisan. As the Manchester Times again reported on October 25th, the Liberal candidate had already dropped out of the running so it was now all about Jack.

Tempers and emotion were running high and it was this sort of atmosphere that Jack enjoyed most, combining the excitement of the challenge and the chase. Working his way around the Shirebrook ward, Jack arrived at Langwith market place around four o'clock in the afternoon where a group of about one hundred miners had gathered to hear Jack speak. Flat caps abounded as Nellie and Jack stood on the steps of the library in the evening gloom of a damp October day flanked by the Labour speaker and Jack's Conservative/Unionist supporters. It had as usual begun to rain and as Nellie began to speak she was heckled from the back of the crowd and…. *"why don't you go back to London where you came from"* was heard ringing out across the square followed by *"what do you know about life down a pit!"* Jack's temper immediately rose in defence of Nellie as the newspaper recalled and the Colonel shouted in an angry tone, *"if you want to take the rise out of someone take it out of me and not out of my wife!"*

Not content with challenging the man in the crowd Jack then walked down the steps and through the assembled miners, who seemed more than a little taken aback that Jack would not just take the abuse, towards the man he had picked out and who beat a hasty retreat across the square. Jack was clearly in the mood for a fight and the meeting dispersed with Jack evidently angry. The day was not over and there was more to come. After tea with the local Conservative councellor, Jack and Nellie walked through the rain for the seven o'clock meeting at Upper Langwith School. Arriving just before seven it was clear that the steam rising from the wet clothes of the two hundred or so miners and local shopkeepers and professionals was mixing with the steam of high expectations. The hall was a buzz when Jack and Nellie walked in to some applause from the front and hands in pockets from the back of the room. Whispers had already spread around the town about the previous meeting and Jack already had something of a legendary reputation about him. Jack, himself, was unfortunately still glowing in the heady mix of emotions that had driven him on before to do so many courageous things.

Maybe this was why he started the meeting by asking if there were any Communists present. Not the most diplomatic start and clearly trying to goad anyone of high temper in the room to have a go and there were plenty of takers. *"Yes, we are here"* rang out from the back of the hall and immediately the tone changed. Jacks supporters jeered, the temperature rose and the atmosphere became tense as Jack took in a deep breath and smiled *"That's good, you are the men I want to meet."* The Chairman, a Major Lemonby and his wife stood up and tried unsuccessfully to quieten the hall down as Jack rose to speak - Nellie squeezing his hand for him to calm down. As he started, a shout with a raised fist came straight at him *"You want chucking out"* and around one hundred miners cheered and agreed. Jack, a bit ruffled, stood his ground and according to the newspaper reports, stiffened his back and shouted *"If there is anybody here who can chuck me out, well come and do it!"* There was a huge cheer from Jack's supporters and sensing an opening like an old fighter he managed to get another verbal swipe in and shouted that Ramsey MacDonald (leader of the Labour Party) had been traitor to the boys at the Front during the war. Not surprisingly the hall erupted with a mass of shouts and raised fists. Jack stood on the stage and shouted back *"yes, yes, a traitor to me and my men!"* At this point a man named Watson shouted *"You're a liar! You're a liar!"*

What went through Jack's mind at that moment we can only wonder. Probably a heady mixture of the need to counter attack coupled with a desire to defend his honour. Watson cannot have had any idea of the life that Jack had lived up to that moment but he saw the result of it marching off the stage towards him - and Watson was not a runner either. Jack walked up to him and looked him in the eye *"Take that back"* was the demand and Watson refused at which point and without any hesitation Jack punched him hard - the first blow knocking Watson to the side and the second saw him hit the ground hard at which point the stewards ran up to restrain Jack. What was amazing was that a melee did not follow. In fact no one ran to Watson's side and Jack's supporters were shocked as if time had stood still. A few seconds passed and Jack composed himself saying out loud *"I am not going to be called a liar by any man. I have fought too long and too hard to be accused of that."* The meeting continued in the quietest calm and the Colonel was given a "splendid hearing" - who was going to shout him down! The next day the Manchester Times recorded:

V.C. Quells Disorder - Interrupter Calls Col. Kelly a Liar - And Pays the penalty

Perhaps the most fascinating result of this extraordinary event was that over the next few days it became clear that a number of men who had served under Jack actually lived in the area. They had mostly been men who had either served in the Inniskillings back from 1915 Gallipoli days or more recently regulars who had been with Jack in Russia as part of the 2nd Hampshires. Interviewed by the newspapers on the character of the Colonel, one man said that he felt that the Colonel was being shockingly treated in Clay Cross and "as ex servicemen whose interests were ever nearest to his heart, they deplored the unsportsmanlike attitude of many men towards him". "In Russia" he went on "the men would much rather appear before him than before their Company Officer, and if his old battalion were in Shirebrook to-day every man jack of them would be at his side." A telling and deep insight into the respect held for Jack from the men he had commanded.

At the end of the day Labour support was too strong for Jack to win this particular battle and he lost the election in Clay Cross - but not before he had taken his vote up from 4,000 to just over 8,000 - a stirring result but how much due to his character and performance as opposed to his policies?

The relationship between Jack and Nellie had been strengthened immensely by the attempt to get Jack into The House of Commons. Failure however left Jack once more subject to his emotions. It would have been reasonable to expect him to settle for a quiet life with Nellie in Buckinghamshire where they now lived but after the defeat in December 1924 we say goodbye to Nellie in this story. Her support for Jack had perhaps been taken as far as she could go. Perhaps he was never going to be able to be what she wanted or needed him to be. Whether they divorced or separated we do not know but at his death and funeral in August 1931 Nellie was not present.

CHAPTER NINE

'I have lived long enough for I die unconquered.'
> *- Epaminondas, who waited until he had*
> *heard the Thebans had defeated the*
> *Spartans on the battlefield before he*
> *ordered a javelin pulled out from his body and died.*

THE END OF THE JOURNEY, 1926-1931

Whatever Jack decided to do over the ensuing years we can be certain that it would not be ordinary and so it was that in an obscure newspaper article dated February 1925 we find a startled report on local golf. Apparently Jack had taken up the game the previous November from a standing start with the maximum handicap of 30 and by the end of February he was playing off scratch! An almost unheard of feat to accomplish in under four months and especially for someone with so many physical wounds. Jack continued to show the qualities of a sporting talent so much in evidence as a young man back in South Africa.

The assumption that Jack was at least trying to settle into a normal social life alongside Nellie would explain why on 31st October 1926 he was photographed at Horse Guards' Parade in London in full dress uniform complete with his large medal group and Victoria Cross. On this special day Jack was asked to lay a wreath on behalf of the Ypres League as part of the then annual commemoration of the sacrifices made at Ypres during the Great War. To be selected for such an honour was particularly special given the numbers of general officers and the like who could have performed this duty but Jack was heavily involved, as Nellie had been, in both the Red Cross and the British Legion and Talbot House or Toc H. Still gravitating towards the light of fame and respect, Jack was able to maintain an image and station beyond the events of 1919. Clearly he was not standing still in anything that he did but something satisfied his thirst for challenge when around 1926 he accepted a job on behalf of Bolivia Concessions Limited - to build a road across Bolivia in South America.

For the next two years Jack Kelly VC, CMG, DSO, could be found sweating and driving his men forward to build a road across the jungle and rivers of central Bolivia. There was nothing more dramatic that Jack could have done to display the truly undeniable force of his restless spirit. He was of course successful, not only in building roads, managing men and making a name for himself as the VC hero from The Great War - but also in contracting malaria.

Returning home in late 1927 Jack entered a convalescence home and he was never to be quite the same again, his health beginning to fail after a lifetime of hurt and punishment. Staying near Bognor Regis, Jack was discovered by Sir Arthur Du Cross who owned Craigwell House near Bognor. It was here in 1928 that King George V had been resident whilst recovering from illness and it was also here that Jack found his last employment as agent for the house. Jack was able to live rent free in Craigwell and found a new role marketing the house to the public. During 1928 and 1929 the Victoria Cross hero of The Great War could be found joking and laughing with the thirteen thousand or so visitors that came through the doors, telling tall tales, still always wearing the inevitable blue pin stripe suit, white collars and shined shoes. As the months wore on however so the wounds of past years began to catch up with him.

It is a mystery having lived near Bognor for the previous three years that when Jack's health finally began to fail with an attack of malaria during July 1931 that he was not admitted to a hospital in Bognor but was once more to be found in Kensington - this time in a nursing home. Why Kensington? Why was he not kept local to the place where he worked and where no doubt he had made many friends since returning from Bolivia in 1928? Could it be that Nellie was still there in his life? Could it also be that it was she that nursed him just one more time as he passed away in Kensington on 18th August 1931? Despite the relationship between them being so tortured by his behaviour and inability to commit it is possible that Nellie continued to stand by Jack right up to the end. Sad, hurt, frustrated but totally in love with the man she had met so long ago in the summer heat and excitement of 1914, we may conjecture that Nellie could just not let go of helping and supporting Jack.

This inability to commit himself emotionally and his consequent indifference to Nellie's suffering no doubt had their roots in his early traumatic bereavements but it also provides a piquant demonstration of the fact that this truly heroic figure, afraid of no man, be he Boer, Zulu, German, Russian or General, still had feet of clay.

Local newspaper reports described the scene of his funeral which was held at midday on 21st August 1931:

"The funeral of Lt. Col. John Sherwood Kelly VC took place with full military honours at Brookwood Cemetery yesterday. The body was borne to the cemetery on an eighteen pounder gun carriage, manned by men of The Royal Field Artillery. A detachment of Grenadier Guards furnished a guard of honour and the firing party. The banners of the local British Legion were carried in the cortege.

There were no relatives present as they are at present in South Africa. Capt. C.M. Guest represented the High Commissioner for South Africa, Mr Ernest Short and Mr H.M. Walbrook represented The Authors' Club and Sir Basil Clarke represented The Authors' Lodge."

Short and sweet and to the point but as news of the funeral spread, a whole series of articles were published not just in Great Britain but also in South Africa as they caught up with the man that they had written about so often before. Suddenly the power of his reputation came home to those who had taken his actions for granted. Various headlines read:

'The death of Lieut. Colonel John Sherwood Kelly VC in a Kensington nursing home has ended the career of one of the outstanding figures of the war. 'Fearless Kelly' was the nickname he was known by in wartime.'

The Daily Express, 19th August 1931

"Lieutenant-Colonel John Sherwood Kelly VC, CMG, DSO died yesterday in a Kensington Nursing Home at the age of 51. He had been suffering from the after-effects of malaria contracted in the Far East. Great gallantry made Sherwood Kelly ("Bomb Kelly" as he was called) a conspicuous figure even among the many whose heroic deeds were an inspiration of the Great War".

The Times, 19th August 1931

In Norfolk though he never fired a shot in anger with The Norfolks, his death was noted by a large full page obituary in The Eastern Daily Press:

'VC Hero's Death - War Exploits Recalled.'

Lt. Col. Sherwood Kelly was awarded the Victoria Cross for conspicuous bravery and fearless leadership in the Great War. He was an acting Colonel of The Norfolk Regiment.

The Eastern Daily Press 19th August, 1931

In South Africa The Overseas Daily Mail possibly said it better than anyone else when their headline read:

"Lonely Death of War Hero, Lt. Col. Sherwood Kelly VC - A Lifetime of Fighting."

Lt . Col. John Sherwood Kelly VC, CMG, DSO one of he most gallant soldiers that the Great War produced has died alone and almost friendless in a London nursing home.

The Overseas Daily Mail, August 22nd, 1931.

A final interesting point to note is the attendance of Mr Walbrook and Sir Basil Clarke at Jack's funeral - almost his only personal mourners. This is most likely due to the fact that when in London Jack had lived at the Club on occasions rather than with Nellie. Stubborn and independent and perhaps alone to the end.

After Jack's death there would have been little estate worth worrying about to tidy up but there would have been his belongings, his uniforms and of course his medals. The former disappeared - perhaps to reappear one day - but the latter resurfaced. We do not know how but it is likely that one of his younger brothers, those same young men pictured with Jack and Nellie outside Buckingham Palace in January 1919, took hold of his medals. Possibly Nellie once more came to Jack to clear his belongings from Bognor and the nursing home and passed them on. Either way for nearly thirty years the medals were lost, but in 1959 The South African National Museum of Military History wrote to a Mrs I.H. Kelly of Marandellas, Rhodesia (Jack's sister in law) transferring £250 to her account for the purchase of Jack's medals for the museum so although Jack never made it back to South Africa, his medals did - with the exception of the White Russian Medal given to all those who fought in Russia in 1918-1920 but denied to Jack - a typically low blow from the establishment.

And so ended the light of Nellie's life and the power and the determination of a once shy and sensitive young man who, driven by the lost love of mother and childhood, became a man for all seasons and all occasions and yet a man who could intentionally hazard all that he built. Tall, grand and yet strong and gritty, a combination of fire and water, at one and the same time he was constructive and yet destructive, able and fulfilled yet wanting and empty. A man of immense courage, able to give his body to be bruised and wounded for a just cause, a man of deep and genuine generosity of spirit and care for others and yet unable to give of his inner emotions to those who loved him back. A man as predictable as he was of contrasting temperament. A man of solid rock built on the sand of his own fears. His life was as full as he could make it and indeed he lived enough to fill three or four lives over and died as he spent his youth, alone, square jawed, staring that straight stare that is displayed in all his photographs - a man who never blinked first, a man who wanted to balance the books wherever he found them wanting, a man for all seasons, to the end a man undefeated.

Epilogue

Wherever possible I have sought to provide the reader with the shadows of historical events that surrounded the life of Jack Kelly. "No man is an island" said Donne and Jack Kelly was no exception - apart from the fact that he was a continent. Surrounded by the turbulence of a world in change, Jack was also challenged by his own emotions, with a volcanic temper venting his frustrations of a life that had not gone his way. He often fought against others, even those on his own side were not safe from attack, but was often just fighting against himself - seeing through battle and war a way of venting a personal anger of cosmic proportions. He was not a man that would stand aside from anything - just the man you needed when a fight was coming - either in a public bar or on a battlefield - but just not the sort of man needed when the relentless spears of injustice were flying towards him.

Jack Kelly was therefore as much a product of his times as his upbringing and personality. If, as educational research has so often shown, we are in so many ways the product of our environment then Jack absorbed much that was good and even more that was painful. His relationship with his father was a mixture of unrequited love mixed with bitter resentment - a heady mix for any passionate young man to cope with. His relationship with his mother was one of unfathomable love ripped away by sudden death. As a consequence, his relationship with the world was to challenge it and ask why me? Unfortunately for the world in his lifetime, it provided conflicts in abundance where Jack was able to ask these questions and many others. Why, what for, why me, that's not right, it's a stupid choice….we can imagine these and many others replete with swearing (one of his undoubted talents) were not only challenging for those around him, but in terms of his service with the British Army totally disastrous. He could fight, oh yes he could fight but it had to be on his terms, in his way and at his speed - which was always at the gallop. He was a giant to the troops that served with him and an ogre to his fellow officers who often did not understand him. Not so much a loose canon as a loose nuclear warhead.

On his journey through life we can pause to understand the historical events that shaped decisions of life and death for millions. We can only pause however, just enough for the reader to explore further and in other works of greater merit. But at least we will be able to see the world as it was unfolding at the turn of the twentieth century and sense the rivalries and uncertainties of national development mixed with the weaknesses of men. "Put not your trust in Prince's nor the son's of men for in them is no salvation," were the words of The Earl of Strafford who had spent his life serving King Charles I only to see that monarch's signature on his own death warrant, just as Tsar Nicholas might have written of George V. Thus Jack Kelly trusted until he saw that trust betrayed, served until he saw that service abused and spoke out when he saw courage lacking in those in high office around him.

He was less a man of his time than a man grappling and fighting with his time. But he was sensitive too, supportive of the common man, loving and passionate and yet playful - his female audience was never disappointed. However his end was unnecessarily sad and painful, his resting place appallingly neglected for many years and his memory largely lost until now.

I have often been asked what that the spark was that set me on the path to write about Jack and to spend so many hours researching and tracking down his life. There was more than one. The first was discovering a book in the University of East Anglia Library called 'The Day We Almost Bombed Moscow.' Whilst I was never a good student and failed to read many of the texts required my Professors, I did read this book and became inspired, at the age of twenty-two, to follow this story and find out more about Jack. To throw away a military career in the face of insurmountable odds fascinated a young man who was himself building a career in the Army - albeit a part time one. The second spark was to find myself almost being reprimanded by a retired Major in a Regimental Museum for wanting to know more about Jack. I think it was the phrase we don't release material about black sheep that did it for me. Rather like Jack, this was like a red rag to a bull and I became absolutely determined to see this through regardless of how Jack came out in any book if I could find enough to produce one. The final spark was discovering his grave in Brookwood cemetery. I had been looking for a bright white headstone but found only a tilting, moss covered and cracked headstone (since replaced by a new one) and felt at that moment that justice needed to be done. Many years later when talking about Jack I was told that I was writing about myself - that was the point of ignition and I have learnt a great deal.

Biographical Chronology JSK

<u>Immediate Family</u>

Father:

- John James Kelly born Newbridge, Ireland 4th June 1850
- Married 30th July 1877 in Queenstown, Cape Colony
- Died 18th August 1926

Mother:

- Emily Jane Didcott born Winchester, England 1st June 1858
- Died 8th August 1892 (The following inscription can be found on a brass plaque in the church of Lady Frere:
  'In loving remembrance of Emily Jane Kelly who died at Lady Frere from injuries on 8th August 1892 from the effects of a cart accident. She was a true Christian woman, noble, fond, loving affectionate mother and a staunch friend.' Signed Jack.

Brothers and Sisters:

1. Emily Nuovo Abele Kelly born Queenstown, Cape Colony 18th May 1878
2. John Sherwood Kelly born Queenstown, Cape Colony 13th January 1880
3. Hurbert Henry Kelly (twin brother) - died 21st July 1893
4. Olive Rebecca Kelly born Buffle Doorns, Cape Colony 10th April 1881
5. Edward Charles Kelly born Buffle Doorns, Cape Colony 28th November 1882

6. Percy Dennis Kelly born Lady Frere, Cape Colony 10th February 1885
7. Gertrude Margaret Kelly born Lady Frere, Cape Colony 5th April 1886 - died 19th October 1935
8. Oswald Claude Kelly born Lady Frere, Cape Colony 5th October 1887
9. Clifford Terrance Kelly born Lady Frere, Cape Colony 26th January 1889
10. Ethel Mary Kelly born Lady Frere, Cape Colony 26th December 1890

Step Mother:

- Selena Collins married 11th April 1894
- Died 1944
- 3 children:
  - Dorothy Elizabeth Kelly born Lady Frere 4th April 1895
  - Henry James Kelly born Lady Frere 29th July 1898
  - Patrick Dermot Kelly born Lady Frere 6th October 1901

Jack Sherwood Kelly

1880-1913

- 13th January 1880: John Sherwood Kelly born Queenstown, Cape Colony.
- 8th August 1892: Mother died in a cart accident.
- 21st July 1893: Hurbert Henry Kelly (twin brother) died.
- 11th April 1894: Father married Selina Collins.
- 1894-1896: Queenstown Grammar School, Dale College (expelled) and St Andrew's College (expelled).

- 1896: Joined Cape Mounted Police (CMP).
- 1896: Fought in the Matabeleland Rebellion.
- 1899: As part of the CMP formed an escort for Sir Alfred Milner on his visit to the Transkai.
- Feb 1899: Dismissed from the CMP for insubordination.
- July 1899: Joined the Native Department, Cape Colony after letters from his father pleading for a job for his son.
- 1899-1902: Served with the Imperial Light Horse and Kitchener's Fighting Scouts in the Boer War - took part in the relief of Mafeking as part of Col. Plumers column, operations in Rhodesia, Orange Free State and the Transvaal. Mentioned in dispatches for bravery numerous times.
- 8th January 1901: Commissioned as a 2nd Lieutenant in the ILH.
- 5th June 1901: Resigned his commission after an argument with his superior officer.
- May 1902: Had been broken to the ranks for insubordi nation.
- Nov 1902: July 1903 - at the age of 22 volunteered for service as a private in the Somaliland campaign in the third expedition against the 'Mad Mullah'.
- 1913: Arrives in Belfast to join The Ulster Volunteer Force.

1914-1915

- 31st August 1914: Enlists in 2/King Edwards Light Horse in London with his brother Edward. Trains and serves with The 12th Service Battalion (The Suffolk & Norfolk Yeomanry) in Suffolk.

- 4th November 1914: Appointed to a temporary commission as a Lieutenenat in The Norfolk Regiment.
- 6 days later, due to his previous service, appointed Major on 10th November 1914.
- May 1915: Volunteers for service in Gallipoli. Various mentions as "Bomb Kelly" during September to December 1915. Assumes command of the 1/KOSBs as acting Lt. Col.
- 21st August 1915: Severely wounded at Sulva Bay and moved into hospital 22nd August until 28th October 1916.

1916

- January: Part of the Norfolks withdrawal from Gallipoli.
- 2nd February: In London and the gazetting of his award of the DSO. Courting Nellie and engaged.
- 26th February: Wrote to War Office complaining that he had received no benefit payments for his wounds received in Gallipoli.
- 22nd April: Married Nellie Elizabeth Crawford Greene at St. Peter's Church, Cranley Gardens, London. Nellie resident at 21 Cranley Gardens.
- May: Serving in France again with 1/Royal Inniskilling but severely wounded & saved by Jack Johnson.
- May: Evacuated to Rouen and then London by Nellie.
- July/August: Recruiting tour to South Africa where the "old fascinations" returned.
- 29th November: Maj. J. Sherwood Kelly receives his DSO from King George V at Buckingham Palace.
- 5th December: Serving as Major with the 3rd KOSBs at Duddingston Camp - letter to CO 3rd Bn asking for a

transfer to 10th Norfolk's as officers and men of the 1st Bn were also in camp who knew him as CO 1st Bn KOSBs.

1917-1918

- 1st January 1917: Awarded the CMG.
- 29th March 1917: Takes over command of 1st / Inniskillings.
- 20th November 1917: Action at Marcoing, Battle of Cambrai, Canal du Nord. Returns home to London.
- 23rd January 1918: Act. Lt. Col. J. Sherwood Kelly receives his VC from King George V at Buckingham Palace.
- March-May 1918: On sick leave as a result of wounds from The Somme and Gallipoli.
- May 1918: Second recruiting trip to South Africa. Complaints about Kelly's use of bad language at East London.
- 6th June 1918: SS 'City of Karachi' left Capetown for England with recruits from South Africa - more problems with discipline and Kelly calling them an "undisciplined rabble.'
- 21st June 1918: Court of Enquiry held by Maj. Gen. Thompson at Military HQ Sierra Leone.

1919

- 11th March: War Office minute stating that "Lt. Col. Kelly is an officer whose tact is not on a par with his gallantry".
- April: Divorce proceedings begin.
- April: Volunteered to lead part of the Archangel expedition to N. Russia.

- 27th May: Landed at Archangel. Parade & comments of Ironside.
- 6th June: Arrived Dvina front line with 2nd Hampshire Bn.
- 13th June: Led successful patrol into the interior and personally kills three Bolshevik soldiers.
- 17th June: Letter of praise received from Gen. Grogan.
- 19th/20th June: Aborted attack on Troitskya / deaths of Captain Gorman and Captain Warwick RE in the column. Telephone call from Kelly to Gen. Graham - "feeling shamefully let down".
- 3rd July: Brought back up the Dvina using Kelley's 'mystery ships'.
- 12th July: 2 Coys deployed.
- 22nd July: Mutiny of Russians & murder of British Officers in Dwyers Battalion.
- 26th July: Ordered to take over command of The Railway Front and to put down the Russian mutiny.
- 26th July: Wrote letter to E.W. Janson Eaton Square, London on situation and his views which was opened by the censor. Challenged and serious offence. The same day he writes to Mrs. Cameron of Minehead talking about Russia again and sending love to his "Babe."
- 31st July: Sent his letter to GOC Vologda reluctant to carry out attack on Red Army Blockhouses.
- Wrote to Rawlinson via Ironside (whereas in the past he had run up against authority in the field, he had always came up against junior or middle ranking officers. This time because of the small size of the expeditionary force it was very fast to be up against very senior officers at General Staff level).

- 16th August: Ordered to appear before Rawlinson as Ironside was away.
- 18th August: Receives orders that he is to be immediately relieved of his command.
- 21st August: Letter from Walshe asking Kelly if he wanted his letter to go to Ironside as a private or official letter. Travels home.
- August: Reported working in The Southern Railway in Blackfriars against the union strikes in London.
- Friday 5th September: Sent first letter to The Daily Express.
- Saturday 6th September: 1st letter published in The Daily Express.
- 13th September: Churchill and War Office responds and all newspapers get hold of the story.
- Saturday 13th September: 2nd letter published in The Daily Express & TUC Congress.
- 19th September: Captain Warwick dispatches his letter on Kelly to Col Thornhill (GSO1) Intelligence.
- 22nd September: Brigadier Gen. Grogan dispatches his report on Kelly to GHQ from his HQ in Archangel - 8 point of Kelly's "lack of balance and insubordination".
- 6th October: Kelly's 3rd letter to The Daily Express.
- 28th October: Court Martial.

1920-1931

- 2nd February 1920: Staying at The Hotel Rubens, SW1. Letter to The War Office claiming expenses for his South African trip in 1918.

- 20th November 1922: Article in a newspaper on his being summoned to Windsor Court for non payment of his gas bill due his being practically bankrupt.
- Start of visits to Nellie's law firm for monthly recovery of shares.
- November 1923: Speaking at an election rally at Shirebrook in Derbyshire when Mrs Johnson, mother of Jack, tells him her son was the man that saved his life on the Somme in June 1916 / article in The Daily Mail 4th December 1923 about this event.
- 6th December 1923: General Election Clay Cross -

Duncan C. (Labour)	11,939
Sherwood Kelly Lt.Col. J. (Conservative)	4,881
Thornborough F.C. (Liberal)	4,488
Majority	7,058
Previous majority	13,306

- 24th October 1924: Thrashes heckler at Langwith in the run up to the election.

- 29th October 1924: General Election Clay Cross -

Duncan C. (Labour)	14,618
Sherwood Kelly Lt.Col. J. (Conservative)	8,069
Majority	6,549

- February 1925: Article in a newspaper stating that in 4 months Kelly had reduced his golf handicap from the maximum to scratch!

- 31st October 1926: Lays a wreath as part of The Ypres League at Horse Guards Parade.
- 1927: Worked for Bolivia Concessions Ltd. He opened up the country, built roads and railways and established a port 6,000 miles inland. Contracted malaria.
- 1929: Worked at Craigwell House near Bognor as the agent of Sir Arthur du Cross, owner of the house, and prepared the house for showing to visitors. 13,000 visited in three years looking at rooms used by the King for his convalescence.
- July 1931: Malaria attack.
- 18th August 1931: Died Kensington Nursing Home aged 51.
- 21st August 1931: Buried at Brookwood Cemetery. Full military honours but no family or Nellie present.

INDEX

Craigwell House, 234
Cranley Gardens, London, 93, 111, 114
Crawford Greene, George, 58-9
Crawford Greene, William Pomeroy, 59-60, 223
Curragh Mutiny, 47

Daily Express, The, 204-5, 236
Didcott, Emily Jane, 16-17
Divisions
    24th Division, 100
    29th Division, 72, 91, 99, 102, 133-4
    51st Division, 125
Duddingstone Camp, 115
Dvina River, 166, 187
Eastern Daily Press, 221, 237
Ekaterinburg, 164

George V, King, 146-7, 149
Gladstone, William Ewart, 43-4
Glen Gray Act, 13
Gorman, Capt. D.T., 192
Grahamstown, South Africa, 19
Grey, Sir Edward, 50-51
Grogan, Brig. G.W. St. George, 184-5, 189, 193, 203

Hertzog, Gen. J.M.B, 138-140
Hill, Lieut. G. E., 194-5
HMS "City of Karachi", 141
Hoare, Sir Samuel, 157
Hotel Rubens, London, 217, 219

Imperial Light Horse, 26-30
Ironside, Maj Gen. Edmund, 166, 187, 195-6, 213

Janson E. E., 200-1
Johnson Jack, 102-3

Kelly, Edward, 40-1, 47
Kelly, Hurbert Henry, 10, 18
Kelly, John James, 11-14
Kitchener, 1st Lord Horatio Herbert, 52, 61
Knox, Gen. Sir Alfred, 145, 156, 160
Kruger, Paul, President South African Republic, 23-5

Lady Frere, South Africa, 11-12
Langwith, 229
Lenin, Vladimir Iilych, 151, 154, 168
Lloyd George, Prime Minister David, 46, 70, 145-7, 170, 220

Mafeking, Relief of, 29
Matabeleland Rebellion, 21
Middlesex Guildhall, 211
Milner, Sir Alfred, 22, 24, 157
Mount Oriel NSW, 59
Mullah, Muhammed Abdile Hassan, 35-6
Murmansk, 157, 165
"Mystery Ships", 187-8

Norfolk, 63, 65
Norfolk Regiment, 61-2, 64, 93
Norfolk Yeomanry, 82, 84
Nuovo Abele, 10, 15

Obozerskaya Railway Front, 200
Oppenheimer, Bernard, 94

Poole, Maj. Gen. F.C., 165
Port Elizabeth, South Africa, 41

Queenstown, South Africa, 10, 94

Reilly, Capt. S.G., 158